PENGUIN BOOKS

ÜBER ALLES

George Mikes was born in 1912 in Sikles, Hungary. He studied law and received his doctorate at Budapest University. At the same time he became a journalist and was sent to London as a correspondent to cover the Munich crisis. He came for a fortnight and has stayed ever since. During the war he was engaged in broadcasting to Hungary and at the time of the revolution he went back to cover that event for B.B.C. television.

George Mikes now works as a critic, broadcaster and writer. His books include *The Hungarian Revolution, Shakespeare and Myself, How to Unite Nations, Little Cabbages, Italy for Beginners, Mortal Passion* and (in collaboration with Nicolas Bentley) *How to be an Alien, How to be Inimitable, How to Scrape Skies* and *How to Tango*. The last eight titles are available in Penguins.

George Mikes is married and has two children; he enjoys getting away from the countryside.

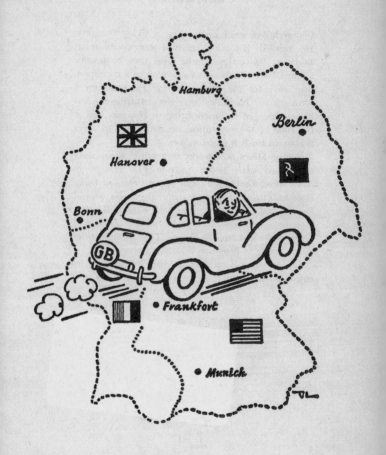

Hamburg

Berlin

Hanover

Bonn

GB

Frankfort

Munich

GEORGE MIKES

Über Alles

Germany Explored

DRAWINGS BY
DAVID LANGDON

PENGUIN BOOKS

Penguin Books Ltd, Harmondsworth, Middlesex, England
Penguin Books Australia Ltd, Ringwood, Victoria, Australia
—
First published by André Deutsch 1953
Published in Penguin Books 1969
Copyright © George Mikes and David Langdon, 1953
—
Made and printed in Great Britain
by Hazell Watson & Viney Ltd
Aylesbury, Bucks
Set in Linotype Baskerville

Contents

Author's Apology

As most Prefaces are, in fact, apologies, I thought I might as well be frank about it. I have a great deal to apologize for.

I went to Germany to write a humorous book on that country but did not find my subject any too humorous. I did not roar with laughter all the time. So I must apologize to the reader who looks forward to finding 'a laugh on every page'. He will not find it. I must also apologize to the serious student: he, in turn, will find my account superficial and altogether too light.

This book, however, is not meant for the serious student. It is, essentially, a book of reportage. I went there because I was interested in that country and I hoped that some others might share my interest in it. What I have seen and what I know about Germany fill the following pages; what I have not seen and what I do not know about Germany would fill a whole library.

Those who wish to study the 'German question' should stop reading at this point. I have to admit that I did not succeed in solving it. But those who care to look around in one of the most interesting and important countries of Europe, not with the eye of an expert but with the eye of a fascinated observer, are respectfully invited to accompany me on my tour – if they have nothing better to do.

I must conclude with another warning. Certain things have changed since my visit – the most important being, of course, that the occupation has ceased and West Germany has become a sovereign and independent state. I made no strenuous attempt to catch up with events because if this little book has any value at all, it lies in its being a first hand account. The date of my picture is spring, 1952.

And now, Gentle Reader, if you are sufficiently braced, we may descend into the depths of the German character.

G.M.

Introduction

I HAVE been living with the German problem since my
childhood. I was born in Hungary, two years before the
outbreak of World War I. I was about four or five when
I heard my father say in the course of an argument: 'No,
you are mistaken. The Kaiser is not God. There is a great
difference between God and the Kaiser. God knows
everything; the Kaiser knows everything better.' I knew
very little about world politics then, but this sentence
stuck clearly in my mind, where it built up a huge reputation for the Kaiser.

My next personal experience of the Germans brings me
up to 1933. In that year German Jewish refugees started
pouring into Hungary and a great number of them,
mostly doctors, came to my father who – as was well known
among the refugees – did what he could for them and
spent an immense amount of money in their aid. I remember one of them quite clearly, even today. He rang our
bell at seven o'clock in the evening and I opened the door
to him. He looked a thin man but was, in fact, a fat man
grown thin. There was a strange look in his eyes. I
thought it was fear; but it was hunger. He was hungry,
and was ashamed of it because people of his class and
status did not go about hungry. At first sight he looked
neatly, almost well dressed, but I noticed on closer ex-
amination that he was in rags. His clean and carefully
pressed trousers were so worn out that his bare knees
showed when he sat down. One of the sleeves of his jacket
had been torn but was carefully, almost invisibly,

mended. And he had no socks on. All my father's patients had left and he asked one of the maids to lay a table in the waiting room and serve high tea for the visitor. I left them sitting talking.

When I returned half an hour later, the German doctor looked happier and the hungry look had disappeared from his eyes. He was sitting in a deep armchair, smoking a cigarette. My father called in my grandfather and asked him to give a few pairs of socks to the German doctor. My grandfather – the mildest and most guileless of men – left and came back a few minutes later with four pairs of brand new socks. 'Will striped ones do?' – he asked the visitor politely, almost timidly. The visitor examined the socks before committing himself and then replied: 'Well, if you haven't got anything else . . . but quite frankly, I should prefer plain ones.' There he was, terrified, hungry and almost barefooted – and he would prefer plain socks to striped ones, free of charge. I thought it was a capital joke. It was only many years later that I understood that it was no joke at all. It was the tragedy of the German character in a nutshell, it was the tragedy of the last eighty years condensed into four pairs of striped socks.

Then I thought a great deal about the Germans during the first Czechoslovak crisis in 1938, when I was travelling from Budapest to London. I thought a great deal about them when the house, where I lived in 1940, was hit by a bomb. I pondered over the German problem when a flying bomb destroyed the Soho restaurant where I was having lunch one day in 1944, and my salad got so full of dust that I had to leave it, thus wasting ninepence.

I thought of the Germans very often when newsreels and documents about concentration camps and annihilation camps were released. And a few years later I, too, awaited their decision with breathless excitement: would they kindly allow us to rearm them?

But it was not these topical questions which really interested me. Why did these kindly and meditative souls go mad, start a planned war and destroy millions of people with the cruelty of savages and the meticulous care of petty bureaucrats? Is there something inherently wrong in their character, or was it all a painful but – from the point of view of their character – unimportant incident, a regrettable misunderstanding? Do they know that they have blackened their names for a long time to come and that there are hundreds of thousands of people all over the world who hate and despise them and never want to set foot in Germany or talk to a German? Do they know this, and if they do, what do they think about it? Is there a German problem for the Germans? Do they have a bad conscience and a guilt complex? Were they really Nazis? Are they Nazis today? What does it mean, anyway, to be a Nazi? Is every other German a murderer, as so many people seem to think? Or are they nice, honest, hard-working, kind men and women who may however kill another six million people if they get the chance?

To these questions I knew no answers. So at the beginning of April 1952 I descended into the depths of the German problem and did not re-emerge until the middle of May. I had never been in Germany before. Now I went there, armed with a couple of notebooks, a fountain pen and two firm convictions:

Being anti-German is just as stupid a prejudice as being anti-semitic, anti-negro or anti-American.

The right policy is to forgive but not to forget. And I also knew that the policy followed by the West was to forget but not to forgive.

Dualism

I FOUND the general picture in Germany so confusing that I feel it is my duty to confuse the reader, too, right at the beginning, otherwise he may find it difficult or impossible to follow my line of argument.

Hitler was a naturalized German subject. He was the worst bargain in history. No other naturalized person has ever caused half as much trouble to his new fatherland. It is true that his naturalization followed a somewhat unusual pattern. Normally it is the new subject who swears allegiance to the country; in Hitler's case it was the country which swore allegiance to the new subject. That was a mistake. The English could have told the Germans that it never pays (1) to deviate from tradition and (2) to trust foreigners too far.

Hitler was a great genius, and he succeeded in achieving the opposite of all his aims. He wanted to make Germany great: he made her small; he wanted to unite all Germans abroad: he succeeded in dividing even Germany proper into two; he wanted Germany to have colonies and succeeded in making Germany – for some time, at least – a colony herself; he was an amateur archi-

13

tect, wishing to build up a new and beautiful Germany as fast as possible, but he became the demolition expert who laid the whole country in ruins at record speed; he wanted to destroy Bolshevism and occupy Moscow: he destroyed Nazism instead and brought the Russian to Berlin and still further West; he wanted to purify the German race, but today more white mothers have black children in Germany than anywhere else in the world; he wanted to make the Germans the master-race and destroy the Jews: he was largely instrumental in establishing a new and independent Jewish state and turning the Germans into the new Jews. You may say that all this is only the result of a lost war; but you may also say that all this is the natural and inevitable outcome of his activities.

Marshal Stalin in his German policy followed Hitler's example. He genuinely dreaded one thing, the rearmament of Germany. Consequently he followed the one policy which did, in fact, bring about the realization of his fears.

All this has been a good lesson to the Western Allies as well as to the Germans themselves. It is clearly too silly to clamour and fight for one thing and then achieve its opposite. It is much more reasonable to fight for a certain aim and for its very opposite at one and the same time and, whatever the outcome of the struggle, you get what you want. This Political Dualism is the new school now flourishing in London, Paris, Washington and Bonn. Let us observe a few details of this policy. The Germans are too dangerous, so they must not build a new army, navy, air-force and high command. But the Germans are on the western periphery of the Russian danger zone, and their country may be attacked, so they must take a hand in their country's defence. From these premises the decision follows clearly: the Germans must be rearmed and kept

disarmed at the same time. They must not be allowed to
manufacture arms because they will soon outproduce the
rest of Europe. But they must be forced to manufacture
arms because otherwise they become too prosperous and
free from the burden of rearmament their competition
will become ruinous for Britain. Whatever the Germans
themselves want to do is sinister and suspicious. If they
refuse to be rearmed, we say: 'These wretched Germans!
Of course they want us to defend them and shed our
blood for their safety.' Should they however accept our
invitation to rearm, then we exclaim: 'These wretched
Germans! Of course they want to take advantage of this
explosive *Wehrmacht.*'

There must be free elections in Germany because we
are champions of national freedom. But an entirely free
German government may voluntarily join hands with the
Russians or may involuntarily be gobbled up by them.
The path is accordingly clear; the new Germany must be
an absolutely independent Western satellite.

The West Germans have been under strong Western
influences since the end of the war, and today they, too,
think on the lines of Political Dualism. They want to rearm because it is essential that West Germany should in-
tegrate with Western Europe, and the price of integration
is rearmament. At the same time they are reluctant to rearm because for them an army is synonymous with war
and the best way to avoid wars is to have no army. They
want to be reunited with East Germany because this is
the natural and honourable desire of every patriot. At the
same time they do not want to be reunited with East Germany because they fear, indeed they know, that unity also
means that sooner or later they will be swallowed up by
the Soviet Union.

As far as their attitude towards the occupation forces

is concerned, that is equally clear cut. The occupation forces should go because the Germans resent foreign tutelage. At the same time the occupation forces should stay because their presence in Germany means safety and security.

To sum up, Western statesmanship with the help of German ingenuity has succeeded, at last, in finding a generally accepted formula for the solution of the German question. The Germans must be rearmed and kept fully disarmed; German industry must produce war materials and must be absolutely forbidden to produce war materials. Germany should be reunited but reunification must be prevented by all means. The British, French and American forces must end the occupation of Germany but they must stay in the country.

Without grasping these formulae no one can really understand the German problem and Western policy towards Germany. I must ask the reader to keep this in mind – and now we may proceed to build up a general picture of the Germans and their fatherland.

First Impressions

I MADE three important discoveries in the last six hours of my *séjour* in Germany – and subsequent experience only served to confirm them. One is about the English, the other two about the Germans.

I discovered in Germany that our own officials at home are polite and charming. I realized for the first time that they have certain engaging characteristics which I had never noticed before. An ordinary English official is not devoted to his work, and slightly detests the people with whom he has to deal. This is an attractive human trait in his character. German officials on the other hand love their work, they are zealous priests of a modern, almighty God – the State – and are fully aware that they are representing Deity. The State exists for its own sake, and the people's only duty is to supply raw material for administration.

Even a German visa – the first German document I saw – is worded with bureaucratic gusto and an eye for meticulous detail. Among other things, it tells you whether you are allowed to cross the frontier once or several times within a stated period and whether you may enter at a certain point only or anywhere you like (provided you choose an authorized crossing point). An English visa merely states that you may enter the United Kingdom, and this brief, concise statement is in any case enough for the Immigration Officer to turn you back. A German pillar-box again contains more information than the average English encyclopedia. The notice on some pillar-boxes even informs you that the aperture is there to throw your letters in. On my return from Germany, I was surprised to see that on one side of English postcards – the side which is quite obviously meant for the address – one could read these words: THE ADDRESS TO BE WRITTEN ON THIS SIDE. 'How typically German,' I thought. 'Only the Germans would print postcards like that.'

My next observation is of great historical importance. I learnt that there had been no Nazism in Germany. In Hungary, after the war, everybody told me about the horrors of Nazism and informed me that they had worked with the *resistance*. The resistance movement – which in fact hardly existed – seemed to have contained eight million ardent and active members. There was Nazism in Hungary but there were no Nazis. In Germany there was apparently not even Nazism. If you try to talk to the Germans about Nazism they dismiss the subject with a smile or brush it aside with an impatient gesture. Not that they are ashamed, or have anything to conceal. They are simply bored. The whole thing is over, forgotten, not worth mentioning. They had heard something about it, yes, but it all happened in prehistoric times. Take as an example two young ladies I met in Germany. One told me in the first half hour of our acquaintanceship that she had an illegitimate child by an estate agent who was now living in Dresden; the other informed me casually that she was a Lesbian. But both refused to talk about the Nazi period – although, as I later heard, one had suffered a great deal from the Nazis and behaved with admirable courage. But now they were only interested in themselves and not in past political squabbles. (This refers to the whole of West Germany, except the Bonn enclave. Outside Bonn, people are interested in everything except politics; in Bonn only and exclusively in politics.)

This is one point where my preconceived picture fell to pieces. I expected the Germans to have a guilt-complex, and numerous theories designed to exonerate themselves; I thought they would blame others – but I found that they had forgotten the whole incident – written it off as unimportant. Or inconvenient to discuss. I do not know which – but this chapter seems to have been closed. They started a world war; killed six (or was it ten?) million people including many of their own; laid half Europe and almost the whole of Germany in ruins. But who are *they*? Herr Schmidt did not start a world war. Dr Gruber did not kill one single million. Fräulein Schroeder did not ruin one single city in Germany or abroad. So why do I worry *them* with my stupid questions? Why indeed? Soon I too ceased to feel that there was a conspiracy of silence. No – we were not being silent over anything important. It was just that there are certain subjects not worth while discussing.

It is not only that most Germans have abolished Nazism from their memories and from the focus of their interest (and this is the last of my initial observances), but they are also ready to forgive us. They are generous souls and bear no resentment against us for their crimes. We ruined their lovely country; brought the Russians into their land; we are foreigners still occupying their soil; we have committed innumerable crimes and injustices under the guise of 'war criminal' (always in inverted commas) trials and denazification procedure, but they are wise enough to know that we must live together in peace and it is no good raking up the past. Although their feelings are strong because a number of injustices really were committed, small people victimized and ringleaders allowed to go scot free, and although a few old-fashioned falsifications of recent history did the rest in creating deep resentments, they are quite ready to forget the past. Not only their own past, but ours too. We kneel in front of them, asking their help and cooperation. They pat us on the back: 'Stand up, my friend, we are considering it. What's your best offer?'

Shall We Love Them?

I MET altogether two persons in Germany who thought in a balanced, logical and unemotional way about the German problem. Both were Germans. I heard many intelligent, brilliant and illuminating things from others, but everybody else I talked to was carried away by emotion as soon as this so-called German problem was mentioned. The English in England have no bitter feelings against the Germans, in fact, they like them better than they like the French and much better than the Americans. There is something paternal in their attitude. And they seem to believe that there's something irresistibly funny in being German. In Germany, however, with very few exceptions, this attitude changes to dislike. This antipathy has nothing to do with former Nazi crimes or anything of the kind. The British dislike the Germans because they have their hair cropped in a funny way; because they eat sandwiches with a knife and fork; because they are formal, stiff and click their heels; and because they work too hard and take themselves deadly seriously. The Americans, on the other hand, always have the past crimes in mind. The Germans killed six million

Jews, consequently every tenth German must be a murderer; no, it is even worse: every German must be one tenth of a murderer. That is a matter of clear calculation for the Americans. Americans feel very strongly against the persecution of races, provided (a) it is white races that are being persecuted and (b) it is outside the U.S. And outright killing goes too far, in any case. Millions of decent and sincere Americans are outraged by the enormity of Nazi crimes (as millions of Germans are, too) but the same decent and sincere Americans are aware that the Germans are good and reliable anti-Communists. Being anti-Communist is the supreme virtue today. All Nazis must be forgiven if they are genuinely anti-Communists just as, some years ago, all Communists were forgiven if they were genuinely anti-Nazis. In ten years time it may be again the other way round, and so on and so on, until one bright boy notices one day that there is not much to choose between a Nazi and a Communist concentration camp. But the Americans believe that they are faced with a dilemma. They detest murder but love anti-Communists. The solution: they make the Germans their trusted allies but go on distrusting them. The French, in turn, feel deep resentment on nationalistic grounds. Their country was occupied, devastated and looted by the Germans (rather than the Nazis – the French have longer memories than the Americans). Now the defeated Germans are better off than the victorious French, and they are becoming stronger and more dangerous every day. And the French are compelled to help them to increase their strength and thus to increase their own peril. The Germans do not like to be regarded as murderers. They are touchy people. Most of them are not aware of the general resentment felt against them, and most of them had nothing to do with Nazi crimes, in any case they were victims of the Nazis themselves – they say. Those who speak of the duties of the individual under a dictatorship should try to carry out these duties themselves under such circumstances before they give lessons to others. The Czechs have a splendid record of democratic government, and what can they do today? If we are murderers – say the Germans, who have heard something about the fact that the world takes a poor view of mass murder – then we should not be forced to rearm. One does not rearm criminals. But if we are to create a new army, then free our generals and clear the name of our soldiers who all fought bravely and obeyed orders in time of war. All these views (except, of course, the British view, the most logical of all) are expressed in violent terms and accompanied by vehement emotions. Solutions? – they ask. Oh, the world is in such a mess, we just cannot find a way out of this quagmire.

Nowadays, in the period of courtship and mating, when we all are vying for German favours but still whisper 'assassins' behind their backs, I feel we should pose the question: are the Germans responsible for Nazism? It is a question which is never asked today, as it is considered tactless to speak about it. People stare into space whenever certain tricky subjects crop up and pretend that the six million Jews, and I do not know how many hostages, are still alive. Well – are the Germans responsible for Nazi crimes or not? My answer is: they are not. I have arrived at this conclusion with hesitation but now I utter it with the firmness of a person who has some doubts about his doctrines. I am, of course, one single voice. Not even a politician, only a writer. Not even a writer, only a humorist. So do not take me seriously. I hold no brief for the Germans, I am far from enamoured of them.

There was nothing new in dictatorship even in the pre-

Nazi era. Internal oppression and external aggression were not invented by Hitler. There used to be dictatorships in France, England, Italy and in almost all the countries of the world, and there is dictatorship in many countries today. So it is quite groundless to say that there must be something uniquely wicked in the German character because they established a form of government which – after all – is or was known to almost all other peoples.

There are several answers to that. First, people point out that the Germans voted for Hitler and consequently are responsible for him. I am not going into the details of arithmetical jugglery to find out whether Hitler received a real majority or not. He came to power by legal means and about half the nation voted for him. But the other half voted against him. And what did the pro-Nazis vote for? Some for a strong hand; others for an extreme nationalistic policy; others against the Communists; others against Versailles; others against unemployment; others against a weak and detested régime; others for militarism, uniform and the goose-step; others for a strong anti-semitic policy. In other words many of them voted for ugly and repulsive ideas and they may be blamed to a great extent. Yet, hardly anyone voted for aggressive war, the killing of hostages, the execution of escaped prisoners of war, and the murder of six million Jews. All this was not in Hitler's programme. The Nazi voters bear a large amount of responsibility; but the voters of 1933 cannot be made responsible for crimes committed six or ten years later.

Very well – one may reply – we have indeed seen other repulsive dictatorships, but the Germans created unimagined new horrors. Dictatorship may be old; but the planned murder of six million people is something new.

No other nation has done it or, indeed, would be able to do it. This reply is simply not true. It is not only the Germans who killed Jews. The charming and 'gemüt-lich' Austrians killed Jews; my former compatriots, the Hungarians, handed them over to the Gestapo and the S.S. but – fearing that the Auschwitz-process was too slow – shot a fair number themselves and kicked their corpses into the Danube; the Rumanians, Bulgarians and Slovaks also killed Jews with great gusto and enthusiasm during the war. The Poles started pogroms after the war. The Russians have killed millions of people regardless of religion since then. Their camps are less scientific than the German but more economical from the point of view of the State. Not very long ago in the Southern States of America, negroes were killed, their women raped and their houses burnt down by heroic fighters who wished to preserve white civilization. And what is happening in South Africa today? 'Almost every day an African is either murdered or robbed, an African woman raped. . . . Police figures show that of the 965,000 non-whites on the Rand, nearly one in a thousand is killed each year: one in a thousand females is raped: and one in every *hundred* is assaulted. . . . It was exceptional to find someone on the Rand who had not been beaten up and robbed or who had not a relative or friend who had had such an experi-ence.' (Peter Abrahams in the *Observer*.) The S.S. wore black uniform; the Klan white nightshirts and the South African Globe Gang wears red fezes. Pogroms against Jews, Armenians, Catholics, Protestants, negroes or people of bourgeois origin were not invented by the Ger-mans. But all the other massacres – one may object – were committed by mobs running amok and were not officially organized. When criminals get hold of the government, everything they do is 'official'. Besides, St

Bartholomew night in France, the massacre of the Armenians in Turkey and the liquidation of about ten million people in Russia (to mention only a few examples) was or is quite official. The Nazi crimes were horrifying; but there was nothing specially German about them.

A further argument on racial lines is to point out the enormity of the Nazi crimes. The number of victims is indeed shattering. But the Germans are efficient people. Efficient plumbers, efficient bureaucrats and efficient killers. Efficiency is not a virtue in itself. I prefer an efficient secretary to an inefficient one, but I also prefer an inefficient murderer to an efficient one. But efficiency is not the real explanation. We live in a scientific age, and pogroms, if they are to be carried out at all, are carried out in that way. The long knives have been replaced by the gas chamber, just as spears and guns have been replaced by atomic and hydrogen bombs. Hitler's crime against the Jews will cling to the German name for a long time – but Auschwitz was not really the product of a special nation; it was the product of a special, scientific age.

Professor Heuss, President of the West German Republic, has said that the Germans had to reject the doctrine of collective responsibility but had to accept the doctrine of collective shame. But the shame, though primarily German, is also a global shame. The shame of humanity. I am ashamed of Auschwitz myself, just as a member of the human race. Szàlasi's régime in Hungary, Antonescu's in Rumania, and Father Tiso's in Slovakia were not much better than Hitler's in Germany.

Britain is the most civilized country in the world and the British people the most civilized nation. Yet, if Britain had been militarily defeated (or the United States, or Sweden or Honduras) and thugs, cosh-boys, bruisers, criminal lunatics and sexual maniacs put in power, I doubt whether our own régime would have been much more attractive than Hitler's. Hitler would have seen to it that it would not. And then twelve years of Nazi education would have done a great deal more.

The Germans, however, must face another consequence. They must face the fact that they lived under Nazi rule for twelve years. They may not be responsible for it but they had it. And twelve years of Nazism and long decades of previous military dictatorship had no edifying effect on them. Their mentality is poisoned and they do not even know it. I talked to many politicians who told me that they had said one thing when they really meant another. Why? 'Because you just cannot say it.' When I was in Bonn – just when the contractual agreement for the end of the occupation and the rearmament of Germany was being negotiated – many honest Socialists told me that they really did not believe in the possibility of reuniting Germany. 'Why don't you say so in public?' I asked. 'Oh, you can't say that.' I heard that one of the party-leaders had persuaded another party to make an electoral agreement with him on the explicit ground that this agreement would not commit them to form a coalition government. When the election was won he claimed that the others must join the coalition as a natural outcome of the electoral agreement. A woman-politician reminded the party-leader of his previous promise whereupon he turned to her indignantly and exclaimed: 'I really did not expect you to take my promises seriously!' Many agreements are still made to gain tactical advantages and not to be kept. The loudest opponents of Adenauer's Western orientation policy admit in private discussion that they consider his policy right and wise. I heard progressive artists fulminating against a certain silly but harmless school of painting and urging that this way of painting should be banned. The Socialist Party as well as the Christian Democrats are organized on authoritarian lines. Most Germans are fully aware that the Nazi Führer was a bad bargain; many believe today that what they need is a democratic Führer and, maybe, democratic concentration camps. I am not alluding to Herr Schumacher or Dr Adenauer. The first was almost a saint, the second is one of the most astute politicians Germany has had since Bismarck.

Imagine that we have liberated the Eskimos, not from the oppression of a régime but from the oppression of Nature. Suppose that atomic energy really can perform miracles in the transformation of Nature, and we have succeeded in transforming the Arctic region into a second Riviera or subtropical climate. Tundra, moss and lichen would be replaced by palm trees; reindeer, caribou and hares by monkeys, elephants and parrots; seal, walrus and whale would now be of little importance to the Eskimos because they would have plenty of chicken, pork and beef. Even then it would not be easy to persuade the Etah Eskimos of North West Greenland that it is blissful to spend Sunday afternoon in a deck chair, having a sunbath. They never thought of it. It was the last thing they missed. For a long time they would prefer fast dogs to fast motor cars. They would want plenty of whale instead of chicken en casserole and bananas and pineapples. The absence of snow would seem disquietening to them and a green environment unnatural. They would be suspicious of grass, roses and canaries. 'Re-education' would not convince them of anything. But if you gave them a chance to find out for themselves, then there would be two possibilities. They would either come to the conclusion that beefsteak à la Chateaubriand is to be preferred to whale-steak à la Chateaubriand, that it is better to travel on the *Queen Mary* than in the best *kyak* and that a modern block of flats is more comfortable than the *igloo*, even if it is constructed of the highest quality sealskin; or, on the other hand, they may set to work trying to use atomic energy to transform their new Riviera into an old-fashioned Arctic region. It is hard to tell.

The Germans are no Eskimos, and we have not performed any staggering miracles for them. But it is not unfair to say that they are, in some ways, spiritual Eskimos, and now we are trying to force pineapple down their throats.

We should give them a chance. Not to rearm but to stand on their own feet. They have been standing on the feet of others for so long that they do not quite know how to do this. We cannot re-educate them because they are more intelligent in many ways than we are. Besides, one has only to utter the word re-education in front of any self-respecting person for the scheme to be doomed to failure. Let them trade, even if they take some of our markets away. They are going to do that in any case. Trust them for the future but do not trust them just yet because they do not trust themselves and they have been accustomed to live in spiritual igloos for too long. And they are German patriots and not English and American patriots as we seem to expect them to be, whereupon we raise the cry of 'Nazis' whenever they think of their own interests and not ours. They are not Nazis but they were happier under the Nazis. They have nothing against democracy but they do not know what it is. They are not less moral than we are, but they have been infected with a disease. Do not condemn them; just let them recuperate.

The Danger of Thinking

IN the following three chapters I shall point out the three most dangerous traits of the German character: (1) they are prone to think; (2) they work hard; (3) they have a very special sense of humour.

Supercilious writers and silly commentators like to remark that the trouble with people is the fact that they refuse to think. They are quite wrong. The trouble with people is that they do think. This trouble amounts to serious danger when people not only think but think logically. The English are a salutary exception. They do not think. And when I say that they do not think, I am not trying to jibe at them. Bernard Shaw reproached the English for not thinking instead of complimenting them on – and admiring them for – it. They do not need to think because they possess robust common sense. Thinking in most cases is only a poor substitute for common sense.

The English dare to be illogical. Illogical, like life; illogical, like God. They do not introduce prohibition but they forbid drinks being served before 11 a.m. and between 3 and 5.30 p.m. Now does this make sense? Of course it does. They are proud of their constitution which does not exist, and pay the Leader of the Opposition to bully the Government. They say they have freedom of speech and expression but censor films and make broadcasting a monopoly. In a logical country you could not get away with this, because it is against clear-cut principles; but in a 'common-sense-country' you say: 'To hell with principles,' and the result is that there is no greater freedom of speech in any other country of the world than in illogical Britain. I once heard a story about a priest. He was visited by his bishop who found that the priest was living in a tiny house and was sharing a bed with his housekeeper. The bishop expressed his painful surprise at this discovery but the priest explained that there was nothing to worry about because, before going to bed, he always placed a wooden board between the lady and himself. The bishop was not entirely satisfied: 'But what do you do, my son,' he asked, 'if sinful temptation overcomes you?' 'Oh,' said the priest, 'then I remove the board.' If you leave the immoral implications of this story out of consideration you must agree, I believe, that this is the only way to think and act in life. The British, for instance, have a high regard for personal freedom; but during the war British subjects and foreigners were imprisoned and interned without trial. The British just remove the board whenever they find it necessary. And they remove it in each case when common sense suggests its removal – thus not killing but maintaining and fortifying the principle itself.

The Germans, on the other hand, do think, and they feel that they must reduce everything to first principles. Everything must be either white or black, red or blue, one thing or the other. This is a good rule, but life and things do not follow it. Everything must be analysed, understood and pigeonholed. The Weimar democracy was a true democracy, a much clearer and truer democracy on paper than ours, and it took itself so deadly seriously that it regarded it as its sacred duty to give a democratic chance to its enemies to destroy it.

The great trouble with logical thinking is that it does not exist. No philosopher has ever arrived at any conclusion by sheer logic. The conclusion always came first, logic was applied afterwards. Thinkers and philosophers have had a greater effect on German mentality than on the mentality of any other nation. But they accepted the teaching of Fichte, Hegel and Nietsche, not because it was true but because it suited them. No philosophy is true in the sense that mathematics are true – not even mathematical philosophy. Fichte was a third-rate philosopher but a first-rate propagandist of German nationalism and German superiority. Hegel was a profound thinker but his teachings are quite illogical and his main theses do not follow from his premises. He taught – if I may condense this into a few words – that the Whole alone mattered and that the component parts and details did not count. So – he added – the State is the only important creation, the greatest of all Goods in itself, and the individual is nothing. He never stopped to explain – or even to consider – why he regarded the State as the Whole. Had he been logical, he would have come to the conclusion that the Globe, or, indeed, the Universe was the Whole and the State, being a Part itself, counted as little as the individual. Nietzsche was a genius, but his admiration for the Hero, the victor in war, the Superman, was never explained on purely rational grounds. He was a snob, a lackey and was afraid of almost everything around him. He was afraid of women ('Thou goest to woman? Do not forget thy whip,' he wrote, but he forgot his whip and never went to women), and he never suspected that lust for power itself is also an outcome of fear. He was probably mad before he was certified. The Germans, these great and clear thinkers, seem to be prone to follow madmen. One madman, Nietzsche, laid down the rules and another madman, Hitler, the paranoiac, with the help of the drug-addict Göring and an insane Hess, found ways of putting it into practice. It is a pity that the Germans attach too much importance to crazy gangs. It all comes from thinking too much. If they were in the habit of using a little common sense, all this could be avoided.

Another great and general trouble is – and this applies also to the British – that whenever people think, they think with their own heads. That is a terrible mistake. One should think with one's opponent's head.

I spent many long hours listening to the debates of the Paris peace conference in 1946. The sharp differences between the Soviet Union and the West were first revealed there. M. Molotov and M. Vishinsky delivered long speeches every day and – among other things – bitterly complained about articles published in the *Daily Mirror*. They also fulminated against private members of the House of Commons who asked offensive questions. The British delegates explained seven times a day that the British press was free and the *Daily Mirror* could write whatever it thought fit; and that an M.P. is entitled to ask the most offensive, indeed, the silliest questions he can think of. The Russians blinked and came out with a new bunch of quotations from the *Mirror* or *Hansard* five minutes later. The British delegates were annoyed and did not understand. But the explanation was simple. The British kept thinking with their own heads and the Russians with theirs. This freedom of the press and freedom of speech business – the Russians thought – was a very clear and well-known British trick, but it was an insult to their intelligence to expect them to take it seriously. That a paper could write what it wanted and an M.P. say whatever he liked? Nonsense. They knew better. Such things just did not exist, because they did not exist and had never existed in Russia.

Confronted with the Germans, the British committed the same mistake. They – with their Allies – arranged judicial trials for persons accused of major war crimes. A trial is a fair and independent procedure in the eyes of the British, and it never occurred to them that the Germans looked at these things with their own eyes. For them – and also for the Russians, for that matter – the judiciary used to be a part of the executive; just another organ of the government. So they – I mean Germans, belonging to all parties – reject the Nuremberg judgements and scoff at them. They all agree that the hanging and imprisonment of their politicians and generals was justified. The Allies were victorious, so they were at liberty to hang whomsoever they fancied hanging. The victor has his rights (see Nietzsche). But why this comedy about 'justice'? The Allies also committed crimes – they maintain – but their generals, officers, soldiers and politicians were never tried. On the other hand the Germans, too, had staged trials at Riom and everybody knew that these trials had nothing to do with justice. So why insist that Nuremberg was an act of justice and not an act of policy? Hanging is right; hypocrisy is wrong. Not only are all Germans united in this view but they pronounce it with righteous indignation.

As long as we go on thinking with our own heads we can defeat and imprison and hang – but cannot understand – one another.

The Danger of Working

ONE of the greatest crimes of the Germans is that they work too hard. The English – quite rightly – can never forgive them for this.

Even in 1952 a great part of Germany, destroyed during the war, had already been rebuilt. But the resulting picture was often a strange mixture of ruins and luxury. In Munich, the first thing which caught my eye was heaps of ruins – with hardly two stones on top of each other – but turned – not into dwelling houses or modest little shops – but into luxury establishments for selling porcelain and furs. Shop windows furnished with exquisite taste and packed with alluring treasures delighted your eyes; but you knew that a few corpses must still be buried under the ruins, just a few yards from the handbags, jewellery and toys. Berlin's Kurfürstendamm had been rebuilt, but many of its houses were still uninhabitable and some others empty shells only. The higher floors might still belong to the corpses; but the street level with its treasures, luxurious goods and dazzling neon-lights was a different story. Kurfürstendamm, though half of it was in ruins, was the richest and most beautiful shopping street in Europe.

It was perplexing and you rubbed your eyes. 'How to get defeated?' – you asked yourself, in amusement or bitterness – depending on your temperament. 'The Germans live better today than the English and much better than the French. Nothing is rationed in Germany. The grocer shops are filled to capacity with goods the existence of which the English have already forgotten. The menus of the restaurants seem almost incredible for the English visitor. Huge American cars pass by with German number-plates.' There is a well-known story about two visitors from Israel, who talk about the situation in Germany. 'I know what the solution is,' says one of them. 'It's all very simple. Israel ought to declare war on America.' The other looks at him in some surprise. 'Yes,' the first one explains. 'We should lose the war and then the Americans would spend millions and millions on us. All our problems would be solved.' The other shakes his head sadly: 'This is no solution.' – 'Why not?' – 'Well,' the other declares thoughtfully, 'what if we beat America?'

The visitor from Israel was wrong. It was not Marshall aid which rebuilt Germany. Marshall aid undoubtedly helped – the gift of a few millions of dollars cannot do much harm to any country – but it was the amazing and staggering energy of the Germans which performed the miracles. Other countries, too, received Marshall aid, but no other country has achieved so much although no other country (with the exception of certain parts of the Soviet Union) had to start building from scratch.

I stayed in a small *pension* in Berlin. A friend of mine had booked my room and when I arrived, at five o'clock on a Saturday afternoon, I found the whole place in an unholy mess: workmen, bricklayers, decorators were rushing up and down, the furniture was hidden under white dust covers, masonry was falling everywhere, while the noise of hammering and chiselling was deafening. I looked inquiringly at my friend who explained, apologetically, that all this mess was a complete surprise to him. He had been living there for four weeks and the building operations must have started only that morning, after he left at 8.30. I told him not to worry on my account; a little noise and dirt would not put me off in the least. Then I went to have a look at what the men were doing. A large room had been heavily damaged and now they had started rebuilding it. A few minutes later my friend and I left the *pension* and did not return till two in the morning, when I saw the proprietress and two servants rushing busily hither and thither, carrying furniture and dragging carpets behind them along the corridor. I was tired, went to bed and by next morning I had forgotten all about these activities. But my friend told me an amazing story. By midnight – and it was Saturday, as I have already mentioned – the builders and decorators had finished their work and then the proprietress and the two maids started scrubbing the floor, cleaning and furnishing the room and went on working till 3 a.m. At eight o'clock on Sunday morning the room was occupied by a married couple with a child and it looked spotlessly clean and very comfortable. This tempo was miraculous. In England the same work would have lasted for weeks. But in Germany it seemed to be normal and natural, maybe even on the slowish side.

It was not only building and rebuilding which was pursued with such energy. I saw many waiters in restaurants at two in the morning and met the same waiters again at eight, serving breakfast. I admire the German tempo; let me add in fairness to ourselves that I, for one, prefer to be turned out from a restaurant at 11 p.m. in the knowledge that all the waiters will have their proper rest.

In Bavaria, Berlin and Hesse I saw people work till midnight. Not only waiters but also bricklayers and decorators. I saw others working as early as four in the morning. Yet all these people jibe at the Swabians and make contemptuous remarks about them. 'Oh, these Swabians,' they keep saying. 'They work too hard.' I visited Stuttgart but failed to detect anything to distinguish the way the Swabians work from the way the rest of Germany works. Perhaps they work twenty-eight hours a day – I could not find out.

I personally have nothing against work. A lot of people from Marcus Aurelius to Tolstoy – in other words people who worked very little in their lives in the ordinary sense of the word – found labour beautiful and exhilarating, and exhorted others to work hard. Carlyle was more logical. Sometimes he found work a bliss, on other occasions a nuisance. In *Past and Present* he wrote: 'Blessed is he who has found his work; let him ask no other blessedness.' But in the *Nigger Question* he declared: 'Labour is not joyous but grievous.' And Carlyle was right. Work is sometimes bliss, sometimes – much more often – a confounded nuisance. I think it is silly to preach to people that they should work because work is pure joy. They should work because labour earns happiness and leisure and there is, unfortunately, no other way of earning them. To tell a man that his work is a pleasure for him is the same as informing him that you do not appreciate his labour. You do not appreciate a person for enjoying himself. Luckily, few people will believe that carrying heavy sacks, cleaning offices and adding up long columns is the greatest blessedness. We all have to work, however, and some are luckier in their work than others. A few again really love and enjoy it. Longfellow wrote: 'Learn to labour and to wait.' The Germans learnt to labour; the British learnt to wait. A fair distribution of burden. The Germans have my admiration; the British all my affection. You must be careful with work. You can overdo it. The trouble with work is that it grows on you. The more you work the more you are willing to work. It may become quite a habit. I am sure that is what has happened to the Germans. Ever since I reached the age of twenty-five, I wanted to retire. All Frenchmen, too, look forward to their retirement with expectation and gusto. The Germans dread it. For the French life begins when working ends; for the Germans when the working days end, life itself comes to an end, too.

One of these industrious Germans told me, with every sign of self-pity, that their habit of working hard made them unpopular. 'Between the two wars' – he told me – 'we arrived in China and changed everybody's habits. Before we came, the English shipping firms had had a monopoly. They went to their offices at eleven-thirty, mostly to do nothing. After lunch they hardly ever returned. Mail boats arrived once a month – so about once a month they prepared all their mail and spent the rest of their time playing golf and drinking whisky. After our arrival they had to work like slaves. They had to open their offices at eight and keep them open till seven in the evening if they did not want to lose all their clients. And they did not like us. Just because we worked hard.'

He sighed:

'The world doesn't understand us.'

I looked at him and then said one word:

'Disgusting.'

He nodded. But a few seconds later his face darkened. He could not be quite sure that my remark referred to the world which didn't understand him.

The Danger of German Humour

THE German lack of a sense of humour has created two world wars.

This is not a sweeping statement but a sober assessment of historical truth.

We are inclined to say that a person has no sense of humour if he (a) does not laugh at our jokes and (b) laughs at things at which we don't. Just as we call a man ill-mannered if he follows a different code of etiquette from ours. The Mundugumor tribe of New Guinea, for instance, eat human flesh – which we do not do – and we condemn their habits; but, on the other hand, they eat very little other meat so they, in turn, disapprove of us. Who is right? I do not pretend to know. But we cannot do better in matters relating to manners, sense of humour and ethics, than to abide by our own standards, as we, indeed, always do.

A lot of beautiful things have been said about a sense of

humour. It is a wonderful thing, people keep repeating; it makes a man much more likeable than his neighbour who lacks it. Such statements usually mean that the speaker, who has an exquisite sense of humour – the speaker always has – regards himself as a wonderful man, much better than his neighbour. But a sense of humour may be a good or bad characteristic. A person who is too ironical – however witty he may be – is often only a coward. He knows that he is a constant loser on the so-called battlefields of life and tries to console himself by laughing at love and beauty. That is why the Anglo-Saxons are so right in distrusting irony. Irony, on some occasions, may be an effective and justified weapon in the fight against wickedness, selfishness and stupidity; but in other cases it may only be the parting arrow of an inferior warrior, with which he tries to assert his non-existent superiority. Even the admirable ability to laugh at ourselves is often nothing else but inverted conceit. You are right in enjoying a good sense of humour; but be careful in admiring it. I am all against it. It makes me suspicious. I dislike humorists.

A good sense of humour – whatever its psychological origin – is the ability to see life in a rosier light. It may make one happier, but this is one's private affair. The only general importance of a sense of humour is the fact that it goes with a sense of proportion. It either produces a sense of proportion or is produced by it. If we have a sense of humour, we cannot consider our affairs terribly and overwhelmingly important. Of course, we all know that we are wonderful creatures, but our self-admiration is at least tempered by the knowledge that we have minor faults. Yes, we are noble, unselfish, dignified (but not pompous), good-hearted, brilliantly intelligent and extremely capable in almost everything; but we are ready to admit that we do not know the railway time-table by heart. An average German would never admit this. I heard long, heated and acrimonious arguments about whether, on a certain journey, one had to change at Heidelberg or not. Both sides used weighty and convincing arguments (except the time-table itself) and the losers, in the end, felt genuinely angry and resentful.

Dictatorship and the lack of sense of humour go hand in hand, because the admiration of a dictator or an infallible party presupposes a lack of sense of proportion. People say that a totalitarian system could not gain foothold in Britain (or in the United States) because these countries have long democratic traditions. This is a mistake. A totalitarian system can be enforced by bayonets and traditions have very little to do with it – although traditions may compel the bayonets to do a more ruthless job. The Czechs, as I have already pointed out, used to have democratic traditions. But listen once to a Czech telling you a funny story and you will feel anxiety for their country. A dictator would have great difficulty in Britain because the British would laugh at him. An Englishman loves his country but he would never speak of 'the beloved and blood-soaked Fatherland of my glorious ancestors'. If someone else did in his presence, he would cast his eyes down and feel uncomfortable; and two hours later – at home – he would laugh. Speak in England of 'blood and soil' and people will roar their heads off. Try to explain that the English have invented all the blessings of civilization without exception and they will regard you as raving mad. Try to launch a movement and suggest that people should greet each other by raising their arms and shouting 'Heil Churchill' or 'Heil Bevan' (this is not intended to be a reflection on these two statesmen, and you may substitute any names you wish) and your audience would call an ambulance. In Britain, excessive sycophancy, whenever it occurs – and it occurs sometimes – is often pilloried and ridiculed. Hitler and Stalin made gods of themselves in Germany and Russia; they would have made fools of themselves here. No – the British would say – Stalin just cannot possibly be the greatest hero, statesman and scientist of all ages; and if he is, he cannot be a male beauty and the best dancer as well. And he cannot have the nicest handwriting on top of it all. A dictator in Britain probably could not be chased away today, as the central power wielded by any government has become too strong for rebellion; but it could be laughed away. Before the war, whenever German troops were seen goose-stepping on British news-reels, the audience was always amused and laughed aloud. In Germany the goose-step was found most impressive; the English thought it was only done to amuse them. Throughout the war I was haunted by the thought that the Germans might use it in a major battle. The British – I feared – would instantly drop their guns and steel helmets and lie about helpless with laughter. Had the Germans tried that, they might have won the Battle of Alamein. It is lucky that Rommel never thought of it. But even if he had thought of it, he would never have tried it. The goose-step was sacred – not to be made fun of. German generals preferred losing the Battle of Alamein.

When the British want something they arrange conferences and talk; when the French want something they argue for it; when the Americans want something they buy it. But when the Germans wanted something they used to fight for it. The Americans bought victory by enormous industrial production and sought to buy peace with Marshall aid. (I am saying this with admiration for the people who were the first to understand a changing world.) Talking, arguing and dealing in various commodities – horses, steel, victory and peace – may generate and develop a sense of humour; fighting does not. And losing two wars to talkers and businessmen fails again to cheer you up and make your general outlook more balanced. War, after all, is fighting. It should be won by the better fighters and not by the better story-tellers. Yet, somehow, it is always won by the funnier and not by the stronger. That seems so unjust.

Not that the Germans do not laugh a great deal. But observe their pleasure and their merriment. The *Bräuhaus* (the *Bierhalle* – or tavern) often looks like a temple with its massive gothic arches. There sits the Germans – with scars on their faces – not simply eating and drinking gallons of beer and yards of sausages but making sacrifices to Bacchus and to the god of Good Appetite. The mood is solemn. A man must occasionally enjoy himself, and they are performing a duty now. Along the walls are little statues on tiny shelves, who all represent saints in the temple – Bacchanalian saints, but saints all the same. One little statue in a Bavarian city is the image of a fat little man who is being sick, having drunk too much beer, and is now holding his forehead and vomiting into his hat. This is supposed to be a joke and a very funny joke at that. It is, in fact, one of the sights of that famous city. The waitresses of the *Bräuhaus* are dressed in gay yellow and green – they usually have enormous bosoms – and their friendly smile expresses approval of your eating and drinking a lot. But, primarily, they do not serve you; they serve higher and gayer masters, the pagan gods and the saints on the wall. The Germans eat and drink industriously and conscientiously under the gothic arches in the shadow of grinning and vomiting statues, and go home after midnight with the gratifying feeling that their duty has been done.

And, of course, they laugh, too. But the question is not so much: *at what* as: *when?* It rather depends on the Calendar. Every German knows that the time of the October Festivals and the times of *Fasching* (carnival time) are times of gaiety. They know for months beforehand that, let us say, on the 3rd October, they will be hilariously happy. They go out to the October Festival and have a jolly good time because they have made a note of it in their diary months before. And then they let themselves really go. They shriek and shout. They sit next to each other, singing songs, rocking rhythmically, drinking beer by the gallon and roasting whole oxen in one piece – one single, colossal joint. The joke is that someone is fat and ugly and dances comically, with a fatuous smile on his face. The joke is that he falls on his behind. The joke is that the musicians are also enormously fat, that they wear bowler hats on the top of their big round heads and play so loudly that no one can hear even his own voice. Strangers dance with one another, strangers kiss one another and smack one another on certain parts of the body where they find, as a rule, plenty of surface for smacking. During the carnival parade the shop windows of Cologne have to be boarded up, otherwise they would be smashed. Not through wickedness; not with malice; only as a joke. All this is not very subtle. They are not Voltaire's spiritual descendants, but their laughter is robust and healthy. Of course, there are many truly witty and enchanting people in Germany, just as anywhere else, but however large their number may be, they are not characteristic of the community. The beer festivals and carnival parades are characteristic. The fat man who falls on his back and is greeted by uproarious laughter is characteristic.

Humorists may not be the cream of humanity; or again, they may. Whatever the case, it is significant that the Germans have produced so very few good humorists. They produce literary giants, like Thomas Mann for one, but he has hardly written two lines which are considered even faintly humorous outside Germany.

Berlin is an exception. Berliners are the only Germans I have met who have a sense of humour in our meaning of the word. Their sense of humour is a little cruel; it is mingled with *Schadenfreude*, often against themselves – yet, they have the above-mentioned ability to laugh at themselves. At the time of the heaviest air raids, the Berliner, and he alone among the Germans, was able to look around in his destroyed city and hearing the scream of a new air-raid warning, remark, looking up at the sky: 'But now they have to bring the houses with them too.' Berliners are very different in many ways from the rest of the people. The isolation of Berlin from the rest of Germany is not only geographical; it is also symbolic.

Historical materialism, although containing more than a grain of truth, has its weak sides, too. Historical humorism – a new science, just invented – is much safer. A great power on the plain – I mean geographically, without natural frontiers – tends to lose its sense of humour, and this is the source of all evil. But the great power on the plain may also lose its great power and the plain itself. So it may learn. I, as the founder of the historical humorism, if I may take my modest bow, will not only admire but also sincerely love the Germans as soon as they produce their own, original Edward Lear. Show me the first utterly nonsensical and truly popular limerick in German and I, for one, shall exclaim with joy: 'The German danger has passed for ever!'

I have no idea, of course, how the Germans will take

this book. It would be utterly unfair on my part to suggest that should they dislike and reject it, that would be a proof or a further proof, of their lack of sense of humour. They may possess the most exquisite sense of humour and still dislike and condemn my book for a number of well-founded reasons. But while in Germany, I was often asked a question by various people which I found surprising. They would discuss with me the book I was planning on Germany and then ask me in a voice betraying surprise, irritation and incredulity:

'But you do not want to write this book in your own style?'

I sighed deeply and replied:

'Not really. But the trouble is, you see, that I have no choice.'

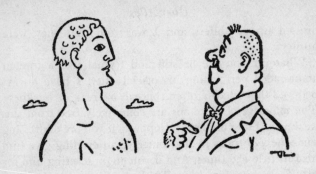

On the Scarcity of Teutonic Gods

SUPPOSE you want to become a German.

You do not need to be a Teutonic god. You do not need to be six feet tall, broad-shouldered, fair, blue-eyed and divine in any particular way. If your laugh chimes melodiously like church-bells sunk in the Rhine, that is all right; but if it happens to be an uproarious belly-laugh, do not worry. If you are brave and vengeful like Siegfried, good for you; but if you are meek and humble that will do as well. If you are lean and muscular like the warriors of the Nibelungenlied that must be good for your health; but if your girth borders on the miraculous and you have a treble chin as well as a treble neck, you are still eligible.

Go and have a haircut. Most people have an ordinary, European haircut but a large minority – I always felt that only they were the true Germans – have their hair shorn off completely, except for a fetching little mane just above the forehead. Then dress up. Dress like a hunter but never go hunting. Or as a golfer but never play golf. Once I saw a whole orchestra in a night club, wearing shorts and hunters' jackets, and I was told that they were Bavarian peasants. Later I saw Bavarian peasants dressed up as golfers and I was told that they were hunters.

Whatever you do, be stiff and formal like a foreign ambassador performing his official duty. I have always believed that 'charm' often conceals a streak of weakness. The majority of Germans are completely free from this weakness. Titles are never dropped: if you are addressing someone 238 times in the course of an evening give him his full title 238 times. And if you go on meeting him for fifty years, give him his full title for fifty years. I visited the house (bombed and rebuilt) where Goethe was born in Frankfurt and the guide always referred to Goethe's father as the *Herr Rat* (Mr Councillor). Not once did he allow himself more familiarity with a man who has been dead for about 200 years. If a man happens to have two degrees, call him *Herr Doktor-Doktor*. One *Herr* will do, but you must say *Doktor* twice. I thought this was a joke, and not even a good one, until I saw 'Dr-Dr' written up on the doors of numerous officials.

Be decent, well-meaning and clean. And believe that cleanliness is one of the greatest of human virtues. Look down upon the French because some – in fact many – of their lavatories are dirty. The French, to my mind, are one of the most brilliant and lovable peoples in the world and even their lavatories belong to the great blessings of humanity. Millions of people may feel superior to them because their lavatories are cleaner than those of the French. I, personally, have a bias for dirt. Not too much dirt – I am moderate in my tastes – but a little dirt. I laugh at the man who spends half an hour a day polishing his shoes and four hours every Saturday afternoon cleaning his car. I like shoes and cars clean if someone else cleans them; but I prefer them slightly dirty if I have to clean them myself. But I shall never make a good German.

Always be well dressed whether you are a millionaire or a beggar. Frenchmen spend most of their money on food and drinks and do not care how they are dressed; the Germans would sooner go about hungry – as many of them do – but they are always presentably dressed. In Germany few people would give money to a poorly clad beggar.

Always explain the obvious and explain it with a dogmatic air as if you had just discovered, for the first time in the history of human thought, that two and two make four, that birds fly in the air and that trains are sometimes late.

Be highly cultured, quote Greek authors in the original, be interested in everything and amass a huge volume of factual information. If you have a chance – and you will often find one if you are on your guard – air your vast knowledge just to show that you possess it. Be paternal to everybody and teach everybody his own business. Do this benevolently, full of the noblest intentions and with the tact of a baby elephant. In Berlin, I deposited all my cash and travellers' cheques with the *pension* keeper, because I hate carrying much money on me (thank Heavens I am not exposed too often to this inconvenience). Next day, needing more money, I asked the lady for some. Instead of handing over my envelope, she asked me: 'How much?' 'Fifty marks' – I said – 'it's for one day only.' She opened the envelope and gave me forty marks. 'Forty is quite enough for one day' – she said, a little brusquely. I did not dare to argue. It *was* enough, she was right. She saved me ten marks. You could have deposited with her (or with ninety-nine Germans out of a hundred) a huge fortune, uncounted. They are honest and reliable. You would get your money back to the last *pfennig* – if only you could pluck up enough courage to ask for it.

How to Breed a Grudge

IF you want to be a good German, you must have a grudge. Or many grudges, if possible – and it is not only possible, but quite easy, once you learn the technique. If you have a slight persecution mania that makes things rather easier. The Kaiser and Hitler had their own little plans concerning their neighbours and the whole of Europe, but they found no difficulty in persuading millions of Germans that they were being encircled by packs of dangerous and wicked wolves. But you can manage even without a persecution mania if you consider yourself the Centre of the Universe. It also helps you to forget the true facts of a case, how any given situation started and how it developed and to concentrate on the momentary position.

Look at some of the current theories. The Allies are responsible for the destruction of Germany. It was they who bombed Germany to bits, and that's the only important aspect of the whole story. Goethe's house was destroyed in Frankfurt, and I heard the ironical question many times: 'Well, tell me yourself, was Goethe's house a military target?' On one occasion I ventured to remark that it was not but it was standing in Frankfurt amidst many military targets. The reply was ready: 'Of course, if you are a Vansittartist ...' The present world situation is the exclusive responsibility of the Americans. It was the Americans who brought the Russians to the Elbe. Maybe others – the British and the French, for instance – have their share of responsibility, but not the Germans. The Germans are only the victims of the present situation, poor lambs. They are always ready to sit in judgement over others and look at matters from a highly moral point of view. When I was in Germany a man called Auerbach was being tried on charges of corruption and embezzlement on a large scale. Auerbach was a Jew. 'Oh, the Jews again' – I heard it said dozens of times. In other words: 'You see what these Jews are like? We killed six million of them in gas chambers and now one of them is again *accused* of these repulsive crimes. You can't make a silk purse out of a sow's ear.' I met a former S.S. woman who complained that the Jews, after the end of the war, were not helping her enough. They helped her, but not enough. The Germans have their answers ready for the Allies' so-called moral superiority, too. 'Racial problems? Well, does anybody in America like having a Communist grandfather? And what about the Negroes?' The same opinion is voiced about concentration camps: 'What about the Russians, your allies in the war? Don't they have concentration camps?' I mentioned to a German woman that it had become very difficult to maintain correspondence with the satellite states. She told me that correspondence between West and East Germany was smooth and satisfactory. I suggested political reasons for this. 'Oh, no,' she said, 'the real reason is that the Russians wouldn't dare to do such things to us. Germany is too big and important.' (Since then, however, the Russians have dared to do it.) Another German lady complained to me in great agitation and almost in tears that the little English boys of the neighbourhood were taken to school by bus while her children had to walk. This, she felt, was an injustice crying to Heaven.

Are these unfair examples, picked out arbitrarily, or are they characteristic? And if they are characteristic what is the explanation of this attitude?

I believe that this attitude is characteristic and it is indeed the worst facet in the character of an industrious and highly cultured nation. The Germans are always offended and everything is somebody else's fault.

The explanation of this phenomenon is that every German builds up a huge reservoir of resentment from birth. An Englishman acts with the same kind of good manners – sometimes tinged with shyness or with the arrogance of unjustified superiority, but still good manners – towards everyone. The Americans again have the uniform brusque and curt manners which they do not change no matter whom they have to deal with. But the Germans have two dozen different manners. They speak differently to the lift operator, to Herr Doktor-Doktor and to the Mayor. Everybody is kept in his place and everybody knows his place. He accepts his position with outward discipline but with an inward grudge. 'I am no worse than the businessman on the fifth floor' – says the lift operator to himself, but when the businessman, who may indeed be no better than he is, appears, he will take his hat off, bow deeply and click his heels. All this starts in the cradle. Children, too, belong to a special class, loved very much, looked after in an exemplary manner but tyrannized into silence and what is considered good behaviour. A child must not talk loudly; must never interrupt adults; must not run about the room; must learn the best table manners as soon as he is strong enough to lift a spoon and fork; and as soon as he reaches the age of two he is generally expected to sit down in an armchair and quietly read the *Frankfurter Rundschau*.

I am convinced that this social tyranny is mainly responsible for the German inclination to accept political tyranny. This resentment, built up in everybody from early youth, explains to a great extent the outbursts of suppressed feelings and also the excesses of discipline for which the Germans are so famous. To me nothing can be stranger than love of power. I have hated dependence all my life. I have never been able to tolerate a boss over me nor could I ever accept my own position as a boss (not that this second position was forced on me too often). I never employ a secretary if I can help it because I hate the idea that someone should be dependent on me and regard me as her 'superior'. If I cannot avoid employing some temporary help I am just as exaggeratedly polite, ridiculously considerate and almost apologetic to her as I am quarrelsome and recalcitrant to my bosses if I have any. In my last job my boss had the same attitude. When I had my so-called annual interview – usually a pompous affair – he was more embarrassed than I and stared into space, not knowing what to say next. He was my boss but could not help it, and I forgave him; in fact, I liked him very much. Now, psychologists may explain that this revolt against authority – whether you hold it or someone else – springs from the same source as the grudging humility of the Germans. The normal thing would be to do your best in your post of life and accept your lot as your due, whatever you have achieved. And if you are not satisfied, try to achieve more by working harder. If you revolt, it makes little difference whether you revolt in the

German way or in any other way. Psychologists are absolutely right. I am not trying to suggest that I am faultless or that we are better than the Germans. Maybe we are worse; I am only trying to understand them.

Another factor which makes the Germans more German than most of us are, is the age-long cult of the manly man. The legend of the manly man is one of the silliest humanity has ever invented. First of all men are usually not manly. Secondly, to tell a man, 'be courageous' is not more sensible than to tell him, 'be blue-eyed' or, 'be tall'. You can tell a man: 'Carry out your duty however terrified you may be,' but you cannot persuade him not to be terrified. He can act, of course, as if he were courageous. He may become brave through fear. He may be more terrified of censure and ostracism than of death. The result from the purely military point of view may be admirable. The generals are not concerned with the finer shades of psychology and do not care a rap why the men stick to their guns as long as they stick to them. But this kind of education has lamentable general results. Great battles are rare, and quite another kind of courage is needed in everyday life. The courage to face your past and future; the courage of looking yourself in the eye; the acknowledgement of your own mistakes and their consequences; the courage to see who really brought the Americans to the Elbe; and the courage to cheer up in the face of the frightful tragedy that your children have to walk to school while the neighbour's are taken by bus.

The manly man is always frustrated. He needs outlets: tyranny over others and tyranny over himself. And he needs outbursts of sentimentality. That is why so many Germans are incurable sentimentalists. I thought that the last war had meant a shattering experience for German artists and film-producers, an experience which stirred and purified them and forced them to reflect on their past. But all I saw in the cinema was sentimental trash played by Hörbiger and Jaray: spring, lilacs, romantic love, whispers in the moonlight and tangos sung in the woods. Half of the world has been burnt down, half of Europe devastated, all our values upset or shaken and the sum total of human suffering in ten years surpassed the sufferings of several centuries, but only one story emerged out of it all: the rich but noble count fell in love with the poor but honest – and, naturally, beautiful, although a shade too corpulent – goose-girl.

Love Thy Neighbour

I HAD a conversation with a German policeman at Mannheim, near the Rhine Bridge. I do not think one could have a similar conversation with a policeman of any other nationality. He was a young man, with large blue eyes and wide Teutonic features, good-looking in a very German way. He stopped me because of my headlights. The streets were rather dark in this particular place and in addition to my sidelights I had my headlights on, properly dimmed. Certain English cars – for some unknown and to me completely mysterious reason – are so constructed that when you dim your headlights, one of them goes off altogether. The car looks like a one-eyed giant, a modern Cyclops; what is much worse, from the distance it looks like a motorbicycle. My policeman, too, was surprised to see that I turned out to be a car.

'One of your headlights is off' – he said.

'I know' – I replied. 'I am sorry, but my car is constructed that way.'

'That I don't believe' – he said, with engaging straightforwardness.

'That is extremely sad' – I answered. 'And I cannot prove it either.'

'Why should they build cars that way?' – he inquired.

'I have no idea. Probably for reasons of economy.'

'But they can't economize like that' – he said, and I believe he was right.

'Doesn't that strike you as quite senseless?' – he asked.

'It does.'

'Then why do they do it?'

'I can't tell you. I should love to, but I really can't. I should say as a guess, since in England we drive on the left side of the road it is sufficient to light up the pavement side.'

'That is quite logical' – he nodded.

'But you said it was quite senseless' – I reproved him.

'And you agreed.'

He had me there.

'However you build your cars in England' – he continued – 'in Germany you should have two dimmed headlights. If you come to this country you should comply with the regulations.'

'I fully agree. You are right. But do the regulations say that you must have two dimmed lights, or only that you may?'

He was a bit perplexed and did not answer. I tried to follow up my advantage:

'Anyway, I have been here only a short time and I am going to leave soon.'

'Oh – you have not been here long . . . ?'

'No.'

'Then how is it that you speak German so well?'

It was the first time anyone had told me that but I did not argue the point.

'I learnt it a long time ago, in Vienna.'

'When?'

'About twenty years ago.'

'What did you do in Vienna?'

'I was studying.'

'What?'

It began to sound like a cross-examination.

'It is no secret at all, but I can't quite see what it has to do with my headlights.'

He was very much annoyed.

'You must have your headlights seen to.'

'I shan't.'

'But you have to.'

'I know. But I shan't.'

He did not know how to take that. A long pause followed, then he asked:

'Then what can I do?'

'Nothing' – I replied.

'You mean nothing at all?'

'Absolutely nothing at all' – I nodded. 'Unless, of course, you wish to take me to the police station.'

'I can't do that' – he shook his head. 'We are instructed to show the utmost leniency to foreign motorists.'

'Well, then show it' – I told him, switching on my most disarming Central European smile.

He saluted and let me pass.

I rather enjoyed that conversation. He showed a large amount of common sense mingled with the same amount of naïveté. His willingness to let me pass was not simply because he could not be bothered with such a trifle; he let me pass in the end, because he remembered an instruction which fitted the situation. It was his duty to 'be lenient', that was quite a different proposition. Life is full of problems, if you know how to find them.

I also liked the engaging honesty of a *Würstlerei* owner

in Munich. A *Würstlerei* is a place where you can get sausages and beer and nothing else. Now the Germans, especially the Southern Germans, are the greatest sausage-makers in the world, and I am the most outstanding sausage-connoisseur who ever trod this planet. I could never pass any of these establishments without dashing in to eat a pair of sausages and drink a glass of beer – although my figure, even as it is, leaves a lot to be desired. This particular *Würstlerei* consisted of one tiny room, with a few chairs and some boards running along the walls – so that you could place your plate and glass on them. The walls were covered with nudes and other beauties, advertising various makes of beer. I was admiring the beauties when my eye caught a small notice which read: 'TOILETTE in the Café Speizmann, next door – in the basement.'

I was deeply touched by this. It was the last degree of honesty, I thought, to draw all the customers' attention to the fact that they had no *toilette* there. It was even more honest to point out that even the nearest toilette – in the Café Speizmann – was in the basement. But that little notice meant even more than that. It was the shining example of cooperation and unselfishness. Why not let the Café Speizmann have a share in the business? A fair distribution of the benefits of a blooming concern, I reflected. That is what the Germans rightly call 'leben und leben lassen' – to live and let live.

On the Road

ONE could write a serviceable handbook on national psychology by studying a nation's drivers. Everything a person says, does or thinks is a reflection of his character. You can study a man's piano playing, his bridge style, his driving style or his way of coming into a room full of people and – if you know how to find it – you have the clue to his character. People have picked on handwriting as a basis for a study of character, for the simple reason that (a) everybody writes while not everybody plays bridge or the piano, (b) handwriting leaves permanent results while driving a car does not always and (c) people are much less self-conscious when writing than they are when they enter a room full of people. But, all the same, the way people drive is worth studying, too.

I have driven in many lands. Unfortunately, one cannot read while driving – a great drawback – so I have to amuse myself at the wheel by observing people's driving habits.

The English have always had the desire to seem to be rude, and then delude themselves by maintaining that their drivers are rude. But they are neither rude nor fast.

They are, on the whole, slow, polite and considerate. But even in England you can witness many surprising things. People who on foot would not dream of pushing one another about, jumping queues, hitting one another in the stomach and treading on one another's corns with special delight, do these very same things when driving cars, and are even proud of it. A thin veneer of good manners falls off some people as soon as they sit at the wheel.

The French are the most reckless and the fastest drivers in the world. But also among the best. To introduce zebra-crossings in France and expect people to stop before them and wait while a few pedestrians amble across in leisurely fashion would be the joke of the century. The car is there to go and go fast, and if the pedestrian cannot look after himself, well, it is his funeral – in the literal sense of the word. Once I stopped my car in Paris to let a cyclist pass and he was so surprised that he fell off his bicycle. On another occasion I stopped for the sake of a young couple, and they were so amused by my innocent naïveté that they curtseyed in the middle of the Champs-Elysées and then performed an eighteenth-century Court dance.

Speaking of the driving habits of various nations, one must mention the Belgians. Belgium is the country where you find the most peculiar drivers. Probably there are as many good drivers in Belgium as anywhere else but there are also far more hopeless ones. In Belgium one does not need to pass a test to obtain a driving licence. Anyone may get into a car and drive away at his own risk. This is all right as regards the driver's risk; I am not so sure that it is all right as regards the pedestrian's risk. If a man is run over and has ten bones broken, well, it is the driver's responsibility. I am a lawyer myself and can tell you that this is absolutely right from a legal point of view. I am not certain it is right from a medical point of view as well – but, then, I am not a doctor.

Watching the roads in Germany you will be, first of all, surprised by two facts. Many Germans drive about in huge American automobiles. Secondly, their own, German-made cars are excellent, beautifully upholstered and fast. All this is held against the Germans. People are biased against them and whatever the Germans do and have and are, is wrong. People do not say: 'The Germans have worked hard, have made their country and themselves prosperous again and that is why they – or some of them – can now drive about in magnificent cars.' No, they say: 'Look at these arrogant Germans – smaller cars just would not do for them.' The excellent quality of the German-made cars is an even graver crime. They compete with our own and French makes on the world market. One day, we expect the Germans not to manufacture arms but to manufacture cars instead; the next day we expect them not to manufacture cars but to produce arms. And we say: 'These arrogant Germans! If they had a little decency they would make and sell much worse cars.'

Their style of driving is not remarkable in the Belgian sense. The Germans are reliable drivers. Of course, they must overtake all other cars on the open roads, but that ambition is more characteristic of the race of car drivers than of the race of Germans. But I have always had the feeling that they enjoy the anonymity which a car lends you – until some unforeseen event compels you to get out and disclose your identity. The German is polite if you meet him socially and if you belong to the class to which he is inclined to be polite. But in a car he is anonymous and at the wheel he feels that he has a chance of giving vent to his resentment about enforced politeness and servility. I said earlier that in France people reacted in the most unexpected way to my courtesy when I stopped to let them zebra-cross (if I may create this much-needed verb). They reacted in an unexpected fashion but, at least, they knew what I meant. In Germany they never grasped the situation. Young mothers pushing prams would not zebra-cross however politely you waved them on. They would not move and looked at me askance and with annoyance. I think they believed either that my car had broken down; or that I wanted to trick them into crossing and would start my car and knock them down – mothers, babies, prams and all – as soon as they were in my trap, in the middle of the road.

There is open hostility between car drivers and pedestrians. The drivers hoot and step hard on the accelerator and pedestrians scatter in fear. It is little wonder that pedestrians try to settle scores whenever they have a chance. An English friend told me the following story. He was going out with his nine year old son. The boy was very excited for one reason or another, and rushed out of the house straight down to the road and under the wheels of a passing car. He was knocked down but not hurt. Naturally, both father and child had a bad shock. The father, however, had to admit, whatever his state of mind, that the accident was entirely his son's fault. But in two minutes dozens of pedestrians surrounded him, all offering false evidence probably in perfect good faith, describing the accident in every way except the actual one. They seemed to be determined to land the motorist in jail. A policeman arrived and my friend still insisted that it was all the child's fault. The crowd was outraged and disgusted. My friend was not only a mad Englishman in their eyes, not only a bad father but also a traitor. A traitor to the pedestrian cause. (They did not know that he was, in fact, a spy. A secret motorist himself, temporarily disguised as a pedestrian.)

A car in the hand of an Englishman is a fast – or fairly fast – means of communication which he sometimes uses recklessly. For the German in many cases it means power. Once I saw a tiny and ancient Austin Seven creeping along the road in England, with the notice behind: 'PLEASE HIT SOMETHING YOUR OWN SIZE.' This appeal was obviously respected. A reckless English motorist is not afraid of an accident and of breaking his own neck; but to hit a minute Austin Seven would be a poor show. In Germany I once had a long conversation at a petrol station with the driver of a huge lorry, pulling two trailers. I asked him in politely phrased questions why he and his colleagues were driving so ruthlessly? The Germans were law-abiding and disciplined people, I said, weren't they afraid of heavy fines and imprisonment? 'Let the other fellow look out' – he replied. Then he added with a broad grin after a short pause: 'We lorry-drivers may lose a law suit; but we always win an accident.'

Racial Hatred

It is enough to spend a few days in Germany to notice that almost everybody is something different from what he used to be. The university professor has turned businessman and the army officer had just come back to Germany from Addis Ababa where he is agricultural adviser to the Emperor. The former teacher has turned haulage contractor and the former banker is now a geologist. This professional upheaval is the outcome of a mass movement of people. Thanks to the war, Germany is full of refugees and this is the cause of countless individual tragedies as well as economic difficulties. Huge masses were evicted from the provinces occupied by the Russians and Poles; hundreds of thousands escaped from the East before and after the Russians arrived; further hundreds of thousands were expelled from Central European and Balkan countries, where many of them behaved abominably during Hitler's heyday and were subsequently made to pay for their crimes. But not only the guilty were punished – the innocent, indeed, the loyal and faithful suffered as well. The very first man I met in Germany – a gentleman of about sixty who looked like a hunter, to whom I gave a lift after crossing the border of Lindau –

had lived all his life in Maribor, Yugoslavia. Now he was living in Baden and was on a temporary visit in Bavaria, but his family had originally come from Hamburg. You may stop someone in a Munich street to ask the way and it is as likely as not that the reply will be in a Silesian, East Prussian or Berlin dialect. All this is the source of a great deal of racial hatred or at least impatience. The refugees consider themselves victims of the war, which, indeed, they are. They have a grudge against those who were luckier than they and who succeeded in remaining in their homeland. It is the duty of these – the refugees think and say – to help them. 'We must be Germans first and Bavarians, Hessenites or Rhinelanders only afterwards' – is their slogan. Nobody dares to contradict such a patriotic slogan publicly; but almost all the local people resent the refugees in their hearts and there is a great deal of bitterness on both sides. The refugees have organized themselves into a political party which has no constructive programme (just like many other political parties all over the world) but under the guise of lofty and high-sounding slogans aims at exploiting the understandable resentment and bitterness of those who have been swept far away from their homes and families. In America they would be called an 'important pressure group' – and, in fact, that is what they are, rather than a political party, whatever they call themselves. The local population keep their mouths shut, do not argue with the slogans about being German first and Rhinelanders or Bavarians only afterwards – and defend themselves as best they can. 'No discrimination!' – the refugees say and everybody seems to agree. But at Frankfurt University Hessenites do not pay fees, while others do. Everyone says: 'All Germans are brothers' – but some Bavarian car-dealers had to dismiss efficient and honest agents because these men offered automobiles for sale in the Silesian dialect and people refused to buy them.

Some of the refugees have succeeded in getting jobs – many of them government jobs as policemen, postmen and clerks. Others live on public help, which they all receive except new refugees from the East who are not recognized as political refugees, and a great number of them live in camps or former air-raid shelters. The conditions in such places cry out to Heaven. And this situation reminds people of their own guilt – guilt in connexion with the refugees and other guilts of the past they all try hard to forget, And this, of course, is the unforgivable crime of the refugees. You can forgive people for almost everything, except your own guilt.

The difference between the various Germans – people from Baden, Bavaria, Prussia, Hamburg, Saxony, Hessen, Westphalia, the Rhineland, Württemberg, East Prussia, etc. – is said to be considerable. The Prussians are of Slav descent, the others are Teutons. Their history and environment are different and their traditions vary to a great extent. I do not know the various German races well enough to paint portraits of them and I do not think it would be worthwhile repeating the well-known truism about Prussian militarism, Swabian diligence, Bavarian slowness and all the other clichés. I wish to make only three remarks in this connexion.

(1). It is probably a favourable turn of events that German race hatred, or animosity, is turned against other Germans. This animosity is not very dangerous, after all, and whenever it becomes dangerous it is controlled by reason and legislation. But the Germans seem to be in need of discharging a certain amount of race hatred just as a car must discharge poisonous gases. It is much better if they discharge these gases on the home market. I am convinced that the Swiss have succeeded in behaving like civilized human beings and living in peace with the rest of the world for such a long time largely because they have the courage to dislike and even detest one another.

(2). The Germans have the reputation of being anti-semitic. I know that, after Hitler, this sounds rather an understatement. What I mean – to be a little more precise – is that Germany's heartfelt response to the anti-semitism of the Nazis was due to a deep and age-old inner need. The Germans certainly are anti-semitic and so are the Ukrainians, the Russians, Rumanians, Hungarians, Lithuanians and Americans, to choose a few nations from an almost endless list. Being an anti-semite, just as being anti-Armenian, anti-Negro, anti-Irish or anti-American, is a mean and cowardly self-justification against strangers or minorities who are different from us. Little boys at school turn against new boys, local people turn against intruders even if these are their relations and 'Aryans' turn against the Jews because Jews seem to be the ideal subject for anti-semitism. They are the chosen people – chosen for that rôle with great ingenuity. But, in addition to the customary factors, the Germans have another good psychological reason for disliking the Jews, just as the Jews have the same good reason for disliking the Germans. Even if we disregard the events of the recent past, Germans and Jews resemble one another in too many respects. German and Jew were denied their national aspirations for varying lengths of time; they were both young and old nations at the same time (the new Jewish State being only a little older than the new German State); they were both minorities – one in Europe, the other in many countries; they were both denied their due places under the sun and both felt the need of con-

stant self-justification. This chest-beating habit developed
in both of them limitless ambitions and an 'I am just as
good as the next man' attitude with all the natural and
often disheartening by-products of frustrated ambition.
They both suspect ill-will and wickedness behind any
criticism; they shout 'anti-semitism' and 'Vansittartism',
whatever is said about them, because they have only too
often very good reasons for these outcries. They have both
learnt to be submissive and martial, sentimental and
ferocious at varying times. They are both accustomed to
swallow insults and then, when there is a chance, to erupt
with the fierceness of a volcano. They both have reason
for many justified complaints, and so they have become
unable to forgo any opportunity of seizing on silly and
unimportant wrongs. They both like nursing their
grudges. Both firmly cling to the basic belief in their own
goodness and the wickedness of others. Both have developed similar vices and impressive virtues, and being so
similar they are not even complementary to each other.
That is the reason, I believe, why Germans and Jews
could get on together even less well than Jews and many
other nations.

(3). It is probably true that Prussians are rude and
rough. And Prussian militarism – a justified charge – is
the crux of the matter. But I rather like them for their
rudeness. Roughness and rudeness may arise from various
psychological factors, but one of them surely is a trait of
honesty and outspokenness. I have always found Prussians
honest and straightforward. Too straightforward, if anything. After all, hypocrisy and flattery may have their
points and courtesy could be defended by skilful arguments; but straightforwardness, too, has some inherent
merits. And anybody who knows Berlin will agree that
Prussian Jews are not different from Prussian Christians.

Kinder people regard this fact as going to prove the utter silliness of race-theories. Less kind people will simply remark that Prussian Jews unite Prussian charm with Jewish modesty.

Anfang
der
Demokratischen
Sektoren

Passport to Pimlico

I USED to think of Berlin as the worst political joke in
history – sharing this honour with Vienna. We were
bravely defending a principle and the result was Berlin, a
heroic absurdity. A city behind the Iron Curtain which is
really a Western city; a Western city which is, in fact, in
the Russian zone; a city, one street of which is in Western
Europe, the next in Central Asia; a city with two curren-
cies and two mayors but one system of communication.
Can you imagine a state of affairs in London in which
many people in Stepney would sooner – and often easier
– go to Moscow than to Shepherd's Bush? It is a veritable
'Passport to Pimlico' arrangement, only more so.

Berlin, indeed, may be a heroic absurdity, but this way
of thinking also shows up the dangers of destructive criticism. It is easy to deride or laugh at these anomalies. But
how could they be avoided? Should we have given up
Berlin or should we give it up now? And in 1944 or 1945
how could our politicians foresee the future development
of Russo-Western relations? Many people are wise after
the event; I personally belong to those who were very

unwise beforehand. I turned towards the Russians with hope and expectations. I trusted them almost as much as President Roosevelt, the well-known Russian agent, did. Now I turn against them with all the wrath of my heart. I feel that all that Stalin did concerns me personally. Up to a small extent it is my private affair. He cheated me in my love – and that I can never forgive.

The anomalies kept staring me in the face. You may board a tram or a U-Bahn, buy a ticket and travel unchecked to the Wilhelmstrasse – which, at first, seemed to me like travelling to Tiflis without a passport. You have the impressive Russian War Memorial in the British Sector. On it you can see the first Russian tank to pass the Brandenburg Gate. In the background you see the Reichstag, destroyed by Göring, its President, and never rebuilt – in fact, redestroyed in 1945. The Russian War Memorial is guarded by spick and span Russian soldiers, in elegant uniforms. These soldiers are one of the sights of the city: they are slightly bewildered, and photographed day and night by American and British visitors. The main Russian radio station is also in the Western Sector, but all the trams, buses and the U-Bahn, in whichever part of the city they may run, are under Eastern control. The State Opera is also in the East, but you can visit it every night, if you please. At the major railway station people will walk up to you offering Eastern marks at a low price. You know that refugees keep pouring in in large numbers, taking all the risks involved in crossing from one side of the street to the other. And also the grave risk of being kidnapped by the Russians and dragged back to their sector in a comfortable limousine. In Berlin you live in one of the most interesting and fascinating cities of Western Europe; and you also live on a Western Island in Turkestan.

Berliners are much steadier and calmer than people in West Germany and less infected by hysteria than people in New York or Phoenix (Arizona). It is natural that this should be so. If you live beside a wolf you are bound to become a little unsettled; if you live at some distance where the wolf may still reach you, you become anxious. But if you live right in the jaws of the wolf, you are beyond caring. You settle down between its teeth as comfortably as you can and stop worrying.

In the Kurfürstendamm I saw the customary mixture of ruins and luxury. The upper floors of many houses were still uninhabitable but on street level you found the richest and most alluring shops in Europe – high quality products, most un-English food-stuffs, silk, jewellery and china. It was a magnificent show, compared with which our own Bond Street looked like a creditable but modest effort. Neon-signs dazzled you by night as you sat perplexed and troubled in a café, almost envying the Germans for their skill and good sense in losing one war after the other. Then a ragged and hungry man on the street stopped in front of your table, eyed the waiter furtively and seized his chance to take the cigarette-stubs from your ashtray, without looking at you. 'There is no market for Berlin's industrial products,' I thought. 'No background, no Lebensraum.' Then I chased away these pompous thoughts, thought of the wretched stubs-collector again, took out my cigarettes and offered him one. He walked away, throwing a mistrustful glance at me. He did not understand; and even if he did, he was much too afraid of the waiter to take a cigarette. He belonged to the stubs-smoker class, and like all good Germans accepted his position. What he wanted was many stubs and not a few cigarettes.

Then I saw the ruins. Whole square miles were completely obliterated. You could not see one single tree in the Tiergarten and much of the rubble had not been cleared away yet from many streets all over the city. You walked in the ruined streets for hours and suddenly a surprising phenomenon struck you. Boards, showing the names of the former and now non-existent streets, had been put back in their old places and little posts erected at street corners; neat little number-plates marked the sites of houses which stood no more. All this was very logical and for one who was trying to find his way with the help of a map, it was very useful. It was also ghostly. And you felt that marking not only the names of the erstwhile streets but also the numbers of the flattened houses was slightly overdoing things. 'It is the result of the German sense of order,' I tried to explain to myself. But the Germans have no real sense of order. They have a sense of symmetry, which is quite different. It was the appearance of order, without being it.

The utter obliteration of certain parts of Berlin and the serious damage to the rest was a disheartening sight. I felt deep sympathy for innocent victims – there must have been many of them – and, besides, no normal person can rejoice at the sight of destruction long after the war. Yet, I never understood the feeling of guilt many of my British friends seemed to feel, nor the apologetic remarks of many Americans. 'It makes me blush to think that we have done all this,' remarked many Anglo-Saxons with horror. I was always astonished by that attitude. To feel sympathy is a natural human feeling; to feel guilty and apologetic is the result of weakness, muddle-headedness or of a very short memory. If anybody ever 'asked for it', it was Nazi Germany.

This half-destroyed and very lively town, situated right in the wolf's jaws, was not only gay and lighthearted but it was a very pleasant place to live in. I grew very fond of Berliners in a short time. Other Germans may be admirable in many ways; they may possess many massive virtues; Berliners may have their faults and failings; but whereas everywhere else in German I felt a tourist in an interesting land, in Berlin I felt at home.

Berlin is still the capital of Germany. Bonn, as a capital, is a joke and not a very good one; Berlin – with the possible exception of Hamburg – is the only non-provincial city in Germany. Provinciality has nothing to do with the actual size of a town. Munich or Düsseldorf, for instance, are large enough and do not need to be provincial; but they are. Berlin is a metropolis. I personally always like large cities. I am more attracted by trolley buses than daffodils. Then, Berlin's air is like champagne. In Berlin one needs very little sleep – even an inveterate sleeper like myself. I often saw people get up in the cafés at one o'clock in the morning, with the remark: 'I am sorry, but I must go. I have two other engagements tonight.' And off they went. I went to bed at two a.m. and I got up at eight. I could not do it in London, but in Berlin I was fresh as a daisy every day.

Berlin is still nearer to the atmosphere of the twenties than any other city in the world. It is 'artistic' in the 1925 sense of the word, and proud of its vices. Or at least not repentant. Homosexuality is rampant both among men and women. I have no idea whether the situation is worse than in other big towns, but it is more openly displayed. Berlin wears its vices in its buttonhole – without a blush and without defiance. People will talk to you about their own odd sexual practices as if they were discussing the weather – which they refuse to discuss, by the way. Berlin, I feel, is not more vicious than other large cities but it is more tolerant. People's sexual life – they seem to hold – is, after all, more or less their private matter – so why not discuss it freely and publicly? You meet no tight-lipped silence, no unreasonable antagonism and old-maidish prudery about the most shocking stories. I hold no brief for vice in general, homosexuality and sodomy in particular. These things have always repulsed me and I could never understand what people can see in a goat. All I am trying to say is that Berlin's viciousness does not seem to be real viciousness. After all, if we knew all the bedroom-secrets of everyone all over the world, I doubt whether we would find Berlin more vicious than Paris or London or Moscow. The Berliner's attitude is the result of many factors, the most important being that they have never settled down for a single quiet and normal week from the outbreak of World War I till the present day.

In 1952 Berlin differed from the rest of Germany in one more respect. In West Germany, people were unable to define their attitude to the occupying powers being not quite sure first of all whether they were allies or occupiers, and secondly whether they wanted them to stay or go. The Berliners were in no doubt. They knew they were occu-piers and they wanted them to stay. Every Allied soldier was the symbol of their safety. And they all remembered the air-lift with great pride. Then Berlin was in the centre of world interest and the Berliners were convinced that the West really cared for them. The days of the air-lift were hard days, exciting days, terrible days. But those were the days.

One night, at two o'clock in the morning, I stepped out on to the street from a night club where all the waiters, barmen, cooks, cloakroom attendants, etc., were high-school students. They worked till four in the morning and turned up in their classes at nine a.m. to carry on like this day after day, night after night. In the street I saw a car with a notice on its windscreen: FOR SALE. INQUIRIES IN THE CAR. And there, to be sure, inside the car, was the owner sitting waiting for the inquiries. I looked around, saw the dark sky and remembered what was around me. About a hundred and fifty refugees were arriving in Berlin every day from the East and the numbers were rapidly growing. Then I heard a desperate shout. What was it? Maybe a joke; or maybe someone was being kidnapped and taken to the Eastern Sector. In a fortnight he would be in Siberia, perhaps, or under the earth; or back in West Berlin. Inside the night club, the Negro band struck up, playing the latest hit from Broadway, and people went on drinking, dancing and flirting with a nonchalance never achieved by Florida millionaires. Someone was ordering another brandy from the waiter who would sit in his classroom in a few hours' time, concentrating on the problems of spherical geometry; a girl was holding the hands of another girl; the man in the car was waiting for inquiries, the car with the kidnapped refugee may be just passing through the Brandenburg Gate. I walked slowly, not quite knowing where I was. Oh, yes, I knew – it could only be Berlin.

A Peep Behind the Curtain

IN the Potsdamer Platz three sectors meet, the British, the
American and the Russian. The square itself is in West
Berlin. It is a strange place: a little terrifying and a little
comic. On the top of a huge building on the Western side
there is an electric news-tape facing Eastwards so that the
inhabitants of the Eastern Sector may be able to read the
news from the free world. The news flashed across is
necessarily scanty and utterly superfluous as everybody
can listen in to Western broadcasts without much difficulty; yet, this gesture seems to annoy the Russians who
have tried various tricks to make the news-tape unread-
able. The Eastern side, on the other hand, is full of
placards, flags, posters, proclaiming the glory of Russia,
the peace campaign and the Soviet Union. Signposts are
distributed all over the square: 'You are now leaving the
British Sector' and 'You are now entering the Democratic
Sector'. The Democratic Sector means the Russian Sector,
presumably because the Russians are so democratic.
There is, however, one remarkable difference between the

two signs: the British sign is in English; the Russian one in German. The explanation for this is obvious: the Russian sign is a little piece of propaganda for Germans; the British sign is a warning to British and American visitors and personnel.

And the warning seems to work most effectively. I have seen many taxis arrive at the Potsdamer Platz, with passengers wearing wide-brimmed hats and colourful ties. The passengers get out, walk up to the sign: 'You are now leaving the British Sector'. Not they. They are not leaving it. They have a good look behind the Iron Curtain – sometimes going so far as to use a pair of binoculars – they have themselves photographed in front of the British signpost and then return home to start work on their book on conditions in Russia.

The Germans, however, come and go seemingly unconcerned. In spite of much discouragement many East Berliners still work in the Western Sector and *vice versa*. And many West Berliners go to do their shopping in the Eastern Sector. The explanation for this is simple. The Russians have tried to maintain the fictitious equivalence of the Eastern and Western marks, but, in reality, in the Western Sectors you can get about four Eastern marks for one Western mark. Consequently shopping is extremely cheap in the Eastern Sector, if you are able to buy your money in the West, which you are bound to do, because it is forbidden to bring Western marks into the Eastern Sector. West Berliners buy bread in the Eastern Sector and many West Berlin bakers – especially those near the sector boundaries – have been ruined. People also go over from the West to buy potatoes and vegetables. They go over to the barbers and hairdressers. The State Opera – situated in the Eastern Sector – is always full of Western spectators because tickets are ridiculously cheap if bought

for Western marks and the performances are of a very
high standard (or so I am told, I am no judge myself).
The East Germans encourage these visits, both to the
shops and to the Opera, but the Western authorities take a
very poor view of this loss of buyers and flow of currency
into the wrong channels. When I was in Berlin Western
newspapers were sending over reporters to note the regis-
tration numbers of West Berlin cars to be found parked
in front of the large cooperative shop near the Brandenburg Gate. These lists were published in the paper but
the number of Western cars outside the cooperative did
not decrease. Cautious and sensitive people parked their
cars in side streets; others just did not care.

Berlin is supposed to be an international city. You may
move from one sector to the other without interference
but millions of Berliners never do. I met many people in
the West who would never cross the sector boundaries
because of fear; and many others in the East who would
not go to the Western Sector because of apathy. The
latter do not want to see how badly off they are; they
know that perfectly well in any case. 'Why should we go?'
an East Berliner asked me. 'We live in a Paradise. Yes, in
a real Paradise, whatever people think.' Then he added
after a short pause: 'At least we are just as hard up for
clothing as Adam and Eve were.' There are children,
seven years old, who have never been abroad – that is,
have never been outside their own sectors.

I, too, felt rather strange at first. A great number of
streets, running from North to South, belong to two sectors: one side is Western, the other Eastern. As I walked
through these streets, watching the other side – which, I
must admit, did not differ from the Western side – I was
very careful not to go further East than the middle of the
road. Till at last, cautiously, I put one foot across and

hastily withdrew it, feeling like a man who has just been rescued from the consequences of his own reckless audacity. Then I met a friend – an English journalist – who told me that he was in the habit of going over regularly. 'I'm not inviting you to come with me,' he said with some contempt, 'because ninety-nine people out of a hundred refuse. They come with me as far as Potsdamer Platz and then declare that they have seen enough.' Of course, I had to accept this challenge. 'I shall go with you,' I told him with nonchalance, and then asked: 'Do you think if we disappear, we shall get a little publicity?' being in the habit of seeing the advantageous side of everything. 'Sure,' he said. 'There will be a hell of a row. But we shall not be allowed to read Western newspapers in Uzbek prisons.' Well, there is a snag in everything, I thought, but I could not go back on my word.

Next morning we drove toward the Brandenburg Gate and reached the Russian – I mean, the Democratic – Sector. Both the Western and the Eastern People's Police saluted us politely, because my friend's car had a British military number plate. Other cars – belonging to lesser mortals – were stopped and searched for contraband. My friend remarked: 'Smugglers take other routes. There are literally hundreds of unguarded crossing-points. If you've something to hide you simply take an unguarded route.' He knew that, the police knew it, the smugglers knew it, but the farce of search had to go on.

Of course, you cannot see much in a short visit. I must refer serious students of Eastern conditions to more learned tracts, the 'I was Stalin's prisoner', 'I was Stalin's Uncle' and 'I was Stalin's brother' type.

Just as soon as you enter the Russian Sector, you realize that you have arrived in a different world. Although East Berlin is a showpiece – the Russians know that many

Western visitors go over to their sector – everything is shabby and poor. After West Berlin's exaggerated – I might almost say infuriating – luxury, the contrast cries aloud. You seem to be able to get a great many things in East Berlin, which, I was told, one cannot get in the Eastern zone proper, but at a high price and of very poor quality. I saw electrical appliances such as lamps in the shop windows and the thin layer of paint was falling off them before they reached the customer. I saw black frying pans, made of the worst kind of crude iron, which looked filthy and disgusting. Shoes were appallingly badly made and ugly. The various textiles I examined in the nationalized shops were so rough and hard that one could almost break them into two as one might break a piece of very stale bread. But, however poor these goods were, there was an *embarras de richesse* in placards, posters, flags and pictures of Stalin. You could hardly walk two steps without seeing a poster bearing the legend, 'We thank Generalissimo Stalin for his wise peace policy' – or something similar. The impression you gained was that of a permanent bank-holiday of a people who had no banks.

At one o'clock we were walking through one of the big cooperative stores and I suggested to my friend that we should eat a pair of sausages. He was quite outraged. 'I am not going to eat Eastern sausages,' he replied.

'Why not?' I asked. 'Have you got ideological objections or are you suspicious of the material they use?'

'I have ideological objections,' he declared proudly. 'I have to draw the line somewhere.'

I have never been too dogmatic so I had a pair of sausages. They were not very good and I had shrewd suspicions that my friend's ideological objections were based on former experience. Once in America I saw an advertisement which read: 'Our Frankfurters are full of ingredients'. The East German sausage was chock full of ingredients, too.

I was under the impression that at least rebuilding was proceeding on a magnificent scale in East Berlin. After all, the East German government could force people to work. They had ordained that the debris and fallen masonry from the Stalin Allee – a long thoroughfare where all the houses were razed to the ground – had to be cleared away before the end of the year. People were asked, in the customary gentle and persuasive manner of the Communist authorities, to volunteer for rubble-clearing shifts – about three hours per day. In addition to the usual pressure and threats, there were inducements, too. People who volunteered for one hundred and three shifts were entitled to take part in the lottery for a thousand new flats. Accommodation is terribly scarce in East Berlin and a flat is a wonderful prize, nevertheless, the scheme was a failure on the whole. People did not believe the Communist promises. They were convinced that the lottery would be faked and flats would go to the 'activists' – in other words to shock-workers and party-officials who are active in politics, not in rubble-clearing. When I visited the sites, about thirty people were working very leisurely and without enthusiasm, obviously bored stiff. But one or two new buildings were already standing. They were formless and ugly, built in the Moscow barracks' style. The building of small houses was forbidden. Small houses encourage 'individualism' which is the Marxist-Stalinist way of saying that spying on the inhabitants is rendered more difficult.

I saw another place where the employees of various big firms were supposed to be clearing away the rubble. They had also 'volunteered', of course, and the site was full of pictures and posters, carrying political slogans about the deep gratitude all Germans feel towards Stalin. Some East Berlin papers had delivered vicious attacks on the slackness of the workers and I thought that these sinister attacks would have speeded up work. But far from it. Two very old women were working there, one picking up bricks and cleaning them with a duster before she handed them over to the other woman who ambled along and put them on a pile about twenty yards away. The first woman was also sorting out old, rusty nails and pieces of twisted iron. The two women picked up and dusted about thirty bricks in an hour. I could not make up my mind whether the general impression was that of slow-motion picture or of a Marx-brothers caricature of an inspired nation at its feverish toil.

Such was the superficial impression one could gather in East Berlin in a day. It was an impression of apathy and tight-lipped silence. Scores of people – about one hundred and fifty – poured over to the Western Sector every day. The refugees had very little to look forward to, because only a small percentage among them were recognized as political refugees and the rest received no support whatsoever. Yet, they preferred to come and starve rather than to stay and starve. In West Berlin papers you saw small news items every day, giving the number of yesterday's refugees and pointing out how many members of the People's Police were among them This news item was of no more interest to the Berliners than another, informing people about the water-level in the Spree.

Driving through the Brandenburg Gate and reaching Western soil again, my friend remarked:

'This is a great fight.'

'Fight?' I asked him.

'Yes, Marshal aid versus socialist economy.'

'Perhaps,' I said. 'It seems to me though that Marshall aid is winning at the moment.'

'It is. But, unfortunately, socialist economy over there will outlast Marshall aid here.'

I could have answered this, particularly by pointing out the difference between socialist and Stalinist economy. But I was not given to arguing at that moment. I cannot deny that I felt relieved at being back on British-occupied territory. We dashed into the first little restaurant and had a pair of free and completely undialectical sausages – freely achieved by a free community under military occupation – with no trace of ingredients in them.

The Jews

THE Jews are flooding again into Germany. Yes, flooding into Germany: going there from foreign countries. And, of course, they're living on the Black Market; on the fat of the land. While Germans are starving, they make a roaring business. Möhl-strasse in Munich is one of the greatest Black Markets in the whole world. They're not making themselves too popular by doing so.'

I received this piece of information from a Hungarian friend of mine a few years ago. He was not an anti-semite, that is to say, he did not hate the Jews any more than was absolutely compulsory in the circles he was brought up in. And I knew that he was fairly well informed. I must admit that I was taken aback and shattered by this communication. I wanted to see things for myself – and that was one of the chief reasons which prompted me to go to Germany. I reasoned that the piece of information received was either true or false. If it was false – well – then it was just one more calumny on the Jews;

but if it was true, there could be no possible excuse for the Jews to go to Germany for the sake of a little, or not so little, profit and cashing in on the misery of others – even if these others were Germans.

As a rule I believe that all medals have a third and fourth side – but in this case I could not see how this particular medal could have even two sides. If the story was true, I thought firmly, what the Jews are doing was unforgivable.

I was utterly wrong in this presumption. This medal, too, had its third and fourth sides. The facts reported to me were true, on the whole; but the action of the Jews has a long story behind it which goes far towards explaining it.

After spending a few days in Munich, I started making inquiries about Möhl-strasse. First I asked a German couple about it. The husband was an 'Aryan', the wife Jewish. The husband who had an irreproachable, indeed, heroic record, told me this:

'Yes, Möhl-strasse used to be the worst Black Market centre in the world. It is slightly better now, partly because the police have cleaned it up but mostly because general conditions are so much better. You can get everything in Germany, the only point in frequenting Möhl-strasse is that goods are cheaper on the black market, as they are smuggled goods. But even today it is impossible to walk through Möhl-strasse without being accosted at every other step by racketeers.'

On that I could check up easily. I visited Möhl-strasse the same day. It is a pleasant little street not far from the banks of the Isar. There are a few shops in it and I had the impression that it was a street of artisans and of people who in England would be described as belonging to the lower middle class. Doing my best to look like a prosperous racketeer, carrying huge packets of dollars in his pocket, I walked through the street five or six times. Nobody paid the slightest attention to me. I saw no one loitering in the street and the whole place looked calm and respectable.

Subsequently, I did my best to dig up the whole story behind Möhl-strasse. It was not easy to find people who were well informed on this subject; and still more difficult to find people who would talk freely and without much bias. But I believe I have succeeded in piecing the story together.

It is true – as my friend said – that Jews had come to Germany 'from foreign countries' after the end of the war although they had not come as tourists or businessmen. They fled to Germany to save their lives. During the war in Poland Jews and Poles fought side by side in the resistance armies. They were good comrades and the traditional anti-semitism of the Poles – which was neither less strong nor more humane than German anti-semitism – was buried and forgotten for a time. After the end of hostilities the resistance fighters returned to their homes, trying to resume their normal lives as far as this was possible. The Jews, rather naïvely, wanted to be reinstated in their shops, houses and other property, but many Poles – who took possession of these properties – did not fancy the idea at all. The best and most efficient solution was to resort to pogroms. Many Jews were massacred – probably not quite so humanely as in Auschwitz. There were few newspaper reports about these pogroms, first because the Poles succeeded in keeping them dark and secondly because the story sounded incredible. It was only the Germans – people believed – who did this kind of thing, not our allies. There were pogroms in other allied and enemy countries, too, though the Jews learned their lesson, and they had to fly for their lives once again, this time to escape the gratitude of their former brothers in arms. It is the irony of fate that they had to flee to Germany. These were the Jews who 'came' to Germany 'from abroad', in order 'to deal on the black market'.

There they were joined by other Jews who had been liberated from concentration camps. Some people told me: 'These were stubborn people; they remained alive in the concentration camps and made a further effort to stay alive even now. Dealing on the black market was their only chance.' I have heard remarks of that kind many times, but the theory is false. There was no need for the Jews to deal on the black market, but it is true that they had an excellent opportunity. They were almost the only people – almost, but not the only ones – who could do so because they were receiving food parcels from the United States and other countries. These parcels meant life for many Jews as well as for many Germans – whatever the price may have been for the latter. Möhl-strasse saved many lives but this result was incidental; it was not established as a charitable institution and however many people would have starved without it, this fact does not place Möhl-strasse on a high ethical plane. It must also be added that Möhl-strasse was not exclusively Jewish – not even on the sellers' side. Other people were engaged in business there: Bulgarians, Greeks, pick-pockets of all nationalities and many others who had been dragged away from decent homes and transformed in the German concentration camps into the 'scum of the earth'. Again others – for instance a large number of soldiers – also made flourishing deals on the black market although their hunting ground was not Möhl-strasse. Then, some decent and honest traders also carried on business there. Finally, Möhl-strasse was only the second biggest black market centre in the world; the biggest was Bergen-Belsen, the liberated concentration and extermination camp.

In spite of all this, Möhl-strasse was prominently – but not exclusively – Jewish. And the Jews, as time passed, differed from other black marketeers in one important aspect. Charity organizations, mostly from America, went on sending them an avalanche of food parcels and clothing. It was a great mistake – prompted, of course, by the noblest wish to help – not to concentrate on finding a new livelihood for these unfortunate people instead of supplying them with a large amount of goods which was bound to find its way on to the black market. As soon as the first clouds of despair, chaos and misery lifted and the Jews found themselves in possession of the most wonderful treasures in the form of tinned foods, dried eggs, dried fruit, ham, butter, tinned milk, etc., many of them felt that they could not act on a plan. Naturally, they wanted to make money and insure themselves against all potentialities; but this was only a secondary consideration. Their primary aim was to wreck German economy. They wanted to avenge themselves and the black market was their deadliest – in fact, their only – weapon. They were full of hatred; their desire was to stab their assassins in the back. Most people find this today an unattractive attitude; but only a few will say that it is unintelligible or inexcusable.

An indignant German patriot told me that the Jews had almost succeeded in their design. He explained to me that black marketeering and currency smuggling were exclusively Jewish pastimes. Ten minutes afterwards, he described a clever way of smuggling Western marks to Eastern Germany. He was doing it himself, to help some relatives over there. When I reminded him of his dictum about Jews and currency smuggling he became most indignant and informed me that (a) his action could not possibly be described as currency smuggling because he was not a Jew; (b) he did his smuggling only to keep his relatives and (c) although he could transfer money legally, too, it was considerably cheaper this way.

What has become of the Jews of Germany? Before Hitler came to power there were 650,000 Jews in Germany; at the end of 1933 almost 500,000 were still living in the Third Reich. At the end of February 1952 about 25,000 German Jews lived in Western Germany and a further estimated 5,000 in the Soviet zone. In addition to the German Jews, several thousand Polish Jews fled to Germany, and many others were liberated from concentration camps, stayed in the country but never registered with the authorities. Their number is unknown, but the total Jewish population of Germany is said to be about 25,000 – that is about 3.8 per cent of the pre-Hitler population.

Those who have studied the fate of German Jewry closely, sum up their fate in these figures. (The estimate is based on the 1925 figures, when Germany's Jewish population was about 564,000.)

Emigrated between 1933–52	295,000
Survived in Germany	15,000
The Nazis killed	190,000
Died a natural death between 1933–51	64,000

In addition to the foreign Jews who have come from Poland or were released from the concentration camps and remained in Germany, a number of Jews returned to Germany from Israel.

It is interesting – and shattering – to compare the pre-Hitler and post-Hitler figures concerning large German towns.

	1925	1952	% *Appr.*
Berlin	172,672	7,000	4
Frankfurt	29,385	1,145	3·9
Hamburg	19,794	1,100	5·5
Cologne	16,093	760	4·6
Wiesbaden	3,200	300	9·4

Worms was one of the most famous Jewish centres, containing the most ancient Jewish community in Germany. In 1934 there were 1,100 Jews in Worms; at the end of the war there were four of them left (0·38 per cent).

What is the position now? Most of the Jewish youth has perished. Between 1945 and 1949 the average age of German Jews was 58 years. This situation had gradually and very slowly improved in the last few years. There are still hardly any Jewish babies. When in 1952 the first Jewish Kindergarten was opened in Frankfurt, this was an event of enormous importance. In 1948 there were nine Jewish children in Düsseldorf; in May 1952 they numbered eighteen.

The number of professional people belonging to the Jewish race is comparatively high in certain fields and infinitesimal in others. In the spring of 1952, there were 260 Jewish lawyers (*Juristen*, including lawyers, judges notaries, etc.) and many civil servants. But there were only very few Jewish doctors. This is explained by the fact that Jewish doctors who migrated in the Nazi period, could settle down in their new countries and practise their professions; jurists could not do so well. So, many Jewish lawyers returned to Germany after the war but only seven Jewish doctors came back (five immediately after the end of hostilities, two later on). There are hardly any Jewish journalists to be found in Germany – where before 1933 the press was alleged to be largely in Jewish hands – and even the important and excellent Jewish weekly paper has half-Jews and Christians on its staff.

There is no official or semi-official anti-semitism in Germany now. One could suppose that Germany today lacks the raw material for anti-semitism – 25,000 Jews just do not provide the need. But the case is not as simple as that. You do not need Jews for anti-semitism. A German girl-student I met told me that she 'did not like Jews very much'. 'Does that mean that you hate them?' I asked. 'Yes, I hate them,' she agreed. 'Do you know many Jews?' I asked her. 'No, not too many,' she replied. 'How many can you think of?' A long pause. 'Do you know any Jews at all?' 'No, I don't.' 'Have you ever seen a Jew?' I went on. 'Not to my knowledge,' she said and smiled. There is, of course, a great deal of private anti-semitism, because the contaminated atmosphere cannot be disinfected in so short a time. But the Jews complain of more anti-semitism than there is, because if a Jew does not get a job or a loan from a bank – the reason he sees is never his own incompetence or financial unreliability but race hatred. Remembering the stories about Jews in Poland who were massacred when they wanted to get back their property, I asked a number of leaders of German Jewry what the situation was in their country. I was told that the restitution of property was proceeding slowly but not unfairly. The greatest beneficiary of the robberies – the German State itself – was a little slow to acknowledge its obligation but acted decently in the end.

There is an increased, but still limited, interest in Jewish affairs in Germany – in the good sense of the word. *Die Allgemeine Wochenzeitung der Juden in Deutschland*, the only Jewish paper in Germany, sells 39,000 copies weekly. Although a large number of copies go abroad – to Israel and 43 other countries – more copies are sold in Germany than the total number of Jews there. Mrs Karl Marx, the editor's wife (not identical, by the way, with that other well-known German Jewish journalist) told me that every time they start a collection to send parcels to Israel, they receive many letters which run more or less on these lines:

'Dear Sir – I was a soldier and a member of the Nazi party. I should like to make amends to the Jews in a modest way. I am very sorry that I am unable to send you a larger sum.'

The letters are sometimes anonymous but more often the writer's full name and address are given. Youth groups, theological societies and other associations often ask Jewish scholars and public men to address them on Jewish problems and matters are discussed freely and with great sincerity. The German press takes little initiative in the discussion of Jewish matters but they quote news items from the Jewish weekly frequently and extensively. In fact, the Jewish weekly is one of the most often quoted of all periodicals. The broad masses of the German people, however, are still indifferent – and I do not think that this is a bad sign. They have their own worries and many of them felt after the war that the Jews were better off than the Germans. The Germans, they said, had no outsiders to help them. It is also true that the Germans had no insiders to gas and burn them – but this minor point was never mentioned.

The Jews themselves are not dissatisfied with their lot. Many of them are ardent German patriots. They observe, however, certain phenomena with great anxiety, first of all the large number of former Nazis in the foreign service, and then the re-birth of the Nazi Party, or rather the birth of the neo-Nazi Party. The party is of small significance at the moment, but they remember that there was a time when the original Nazi Party was also only a small and insignificant movement.

Socially there is not much contact between Jews and Aryans except for those Jews who are in the public service. The Jews retire into newly built, self-made ghettos and closely guard their walls from within; it is true that not many attempts are made to force these walls from without. They still have to face the remnants – and more than the remnants – of anti-semitism, and they smell anti-semitism even when there is not a sign of it. The German Jews are Germans like the others – often even more so. They nurse their grudge – but as it happens, their grudge is the most atrocious crime ever committed in history. A few of them wish to leave Germany but others have fled to Germany to save their lives. Most of the German Jews will stay in Germany and regard themselves as faithful German patriots, which they really are, and quite a few others have returned from Israel because life is easier, butter cheaper, and meat more plentiful in Frankfurt than in Tel-Aviv.

Bonn

BONN is the capital village of Germany. It would be difficult to speak of it as her capital city although it has 120,000 inhabitants. It is a charming university town on the Rhine and its surroundings with the famous seven hills, including the beautiful Drachenfels (Dragon's Crag) are truly enchanting. There would be nothing wrong with Bonn as long as it remained a university town. But as soon as it tries to pose as a capital city, its dreary provinciality and its parochial puniness cry aloud. It is not so much its size which makes it a village as its atmosphere, its people, and, so to speak, its metaphorical large hat on a small head. Greatness has very little to do with actual size. We have all seen gigantic dwarfs; but Bonn is an undersized giant, a minute colossus – wearing large and much too loose riding boots and a charming, simple peasant-woman's bonnet at the same time.

At first sight you will find Bonn beautiful – as all other small towns in the Rhine valley. Its Cathedral is a slightly improved parish church – but again, almost all parish churches are beautiful in the Rhine valley. Its railway station is like that of Maidenhead, only much smaller. I arrived in Bonn on a Sunday afternoon. Thousands of local people were walking up and down the main street, greeting one another with great formality and gaping at each other. The whole scene rather reminded me of my native village of Siklos (which has about 6,000 inhabitants and is not the capital of Hungary).

The rhythm of life is exasperatingly slow. Tomorrow will be another day; after Saturday another week; after New Year's Eve another year; and in a short span of 47 years another century – so why hurry? In Frankfurt you can buy a London morning paper at 10 a.m. and sometimes earlier, but only two or three days old English papers reach Bonn and most newsagents do not even know when to expect them. The local papers are on sale early in the morning. You may learn from the large headlines of those local papers that Beuel (a neighbouring village) has been elevated to the status of a town – and why should good and decent people possibly want to know what is happening in Egypt or Indo-China? Frankfurt, too, is provincial enough; but it is a large city and Germany's ancient capital. It was one of the several cities with a claim to becoming the Federal Republic's new capital. Why was Bonn chosen and not Frankfurt? Well, Frankfurt was the capital of the Americans and, of course, the new German Government did not wish to stay in the same city. A few wicked people have suggested another possible explanation: Herr Adenauer, the Chancellor, used to live near Bonn and not near Frankfurt.

Beethoven was born in Bonn and his birth-house is open to the public as a museum. There are chemist-shops, wine-shops and even soaps named after him but somehow, in Bonn, I gained the impression that Beethoven was not the world's greatest composer, only a worthy local celebrity whose name has spread as far as Koblenz and Aachen.

Bonn, at the same time, has an unreal atmosphere. People, outside Bonn as well as the native Rhinelanders, are not really interested in politics; those thousands of politicians, diplomats, Members of Parliament, journalists and Americans, British and French officials who came to Bonn a few years ago, are interested in nothing else. From dawn to dusk the talk is of politics, speeches, plans, rumours and intrigues. They live, as it were, in a different medium from that inhabited by the rest of the German people. Bonn is much more isolated from the rest of Germany than Berlin.

These thousands of strange people – officials, diplomats and members of Parliament – were deposited with a bang among these peaceful Rhinelanders. Accommodation is scarce everywhere in Germany but in Bonn it has become an agonizing problem although the Germans with their customary industry and amazing ability performed miracles here, too. The new *Bundeshaus*, the House of Parliament, is the most modern building in the place. It is angular and streamlined and gives the impression of being a transition stage between a precocious baby skyscraper and a glorified pre-fab. The building itself is shared by the Legislative Assembly of the Federal Republic and a restaurant in private hands. The restaurant is open to the public – and so is the Parliament.

The *Bundestag* – the Lower House – sits in a large and spacious chamber. It is amphitheatrical and not unlike the sitting chambers of other Parliaments on the Continent. The deputies sit in school-benches – and very modern school-benches at that. Behind the Speaker – the President – you see the coats of arms of the twelve Federal

Republics and of Berlin. On his left and right there are two enclosures, one for members of the *Bundesrat*, the Upper House, the other for members of the government. In the latter enclosure, the first row is reserved for ministers, the second for secretaries of state and the third for officials. When I visited the *Bundestag* the sittings were prolonged and dull, so my report on it must be unrepresentative (unless, of course, it is representative). Members paid little attention to the orators – who speak from a rostrum, into four microphones. Members were reading their local papers or letters received, while the orators read their prepared speeches. All the speeches followed strict party lines and most of the orators seemed to be just as bored by them as the listeners, if those present may be described as such. But, at least, most speeches were gratifyingly short, rarely longer than two or three minutes. One single speech was delivered with great gusto, vivacity and a blazing inner fire – that one lasted only thirty seconds. As far as the contents of the speeches is concerned . . . well, one of Britain's greatest historians was sitting next to me at one sitting. He listened carefully for about an hour and then dragged me out to the corridor exclaiming: 'This is not history; this is archaeology! . . .' I believe this remark was unfair; but it was what at least one expert felt about it.

The deputy-speaker – the vice-president – Dr Carlo Schmid took the chair. He addressed the House – as all the other deputies did – 'Meine Damen und Herren'. Herr Schmid is a doctrinaire socialist, more of a professor and a dreamer than a practical politician, a man of high intellect and integrity. In spite of his great qualities, his popularity is based on a remark he once made, which was related to me at least fifty times in Germany. Herr Schmid is an enormously fat man. Once he went to visit a colleague's wife and her new-born baby in a maternity hospital. He was asked to wait a few minutes in the corridor. He sat down on a bench and although many babies were brought out from the various rooms he was duly forgotten. After a while a nurse noticed him and asked: 'Excuse me, sir, are you expecting a baby?' Upon which Herr Schmid replied: 'Oh, no, I am always as fat as that.'

Looking from the window of the press-gallery of the *Bundestag*, on my right I saw a courtyard where a woman was hanging out her husband's pants on a string, paying much less attention to the proceedings of the House than the House did to hers. On my left, I could see the large and pleasant terrace of the restaurant, full of deputies, journalists and outside guests. From the terrace you have a good view of the Chamber, and waiters are always prepared to explain to their customers who's who inside, sometimes pointing out the higher dignitaries. People on the terrace are in a fortunate position because the ministers' enclosure is next to the window. Ministers seem to pay no attention to their admirers or sightseers, but it struck me that one or two of them seemed to take care to be always in full view of the spectators.

The people of Bonn are not really interested in all this. They take a certain pride in their city's promotion but they think it is natural. On the other hand, they resent the intrusion of all these strangers who, in turn, do their best to get away from Bonn as often and for as long a time as possible. The attitude of the Bonn people is not anger, only mild bewilderment. They are incapable of anger, they are half asleep.

I hasten to add that they cannot help being half asleep. Nobody can be quite awake in Bonn. This fact has nothing to do with the original character-traits of the native inhabitants; it is a consequence of the climate. Bonn is said to have the worst climate in Germany. It was the Ministry of Finance which first complained that all its employees kept falling asleep or acting as if they were asleep, but soon all the other newcomers noticed similar phenomena. It is just very difficult to remain wide awake in Bonn. Chemists do a roaring trade in all sorts of stimulants, but nothing helps. Bonn's climate is maritime, very wet and it lies low (not quite 200 feet above sea level). The climate of the so-called Bonn-enclosure is oppressive. I have read long and involved scientific treatises trying to explain why all young people become very nervous and tired in Bonn. (I am not as young as I was, so I became tired but not nervous.) There it was also explained that old people live long in this climate but I believe – although I am no expert on the subject – that old people live long in any climate, in fact, the older they are, the longer they live.

I think what the experts actually meant was that if people succeeded at all in growing old in this climate, they remain full of energy and vivacity. Herr Adenauer, although he grew old outside the Bonn enclosure, is held up as a convincing proof of this theory. He is an old gentleman, but an amazingly young old generation. This is just a final touch to the picture of Bonn, Germany's capital village, with its parochial outlook and its buoyant and boyish Chancellor of advanced years and its nervous, tired and permanently sleepy other functionaries under seventy.

The Social Nationalists

THE outstanding political problems of Germany are: (1) German unity, closely related with the problem of Russo-German relations; (2) rearmament – closely related to Germany's position in Europe; (3) economic questions, closely related again to all political problems.

I do not wish to expound my own view on Germany's political problems. I am no politician; and my views carry as little weight as though I were a politician. In the forthcoming chapters I shall let some representative Germans speak. I shall not give their names because in most cases they spoke to me with great sincerity and expressed views they would not have proclaimed in public. But in each case I have stuck to the views and utterances of one single person and have not concocted synthetic interviews, even if this method meant the sacrifice of certain interesting and original points. In every case I have tried to choose people who were faithful followers of their own party but who had the courage to form their own views and keep them secret.

This ability to keep your own views secret and have the courage of other people's convictions made a deep, and – needless to deny – unfavourable impression on me. It happened on many occasions that a man expressed strong views of one kind or another and added: 'But this, of course, is strictly between us.' When asked the reason for this secrecy, they gave varying answers. One was afraid of voicing unorthodox views because he was holding high and responsible position in his party; the other thought it was disloyal not to follow the party line – without explaining, however, how the real wishes of the majority of party members could be ascertained if they are all supposed to keep their convictions to themselves; the third openly admitted that the party line he followed was wrong to his mind but was excellent for vote-catching; the fourth simply glared at me – he was accustomed to living in a country where nobody was in the habit of declaring personal views. Up to 1945 he had followed the orders of a Nazi dictator, now he followed the orders of a democratic dictator of his own choice.

Finally, before coming to my interviews, I should like to say a word about the party whom I have called 'Social Nationalists'. I did not want to imply that the Social Nationalists are a rehash of the National Socialists. Nothing could be more unfair and farther from the truth. I only wanted to say that they try to be as good Socialists and as good Nationalists at one and the same time as is possible. Most Socialists would vehemently contradict the suggestion that they are nationalists. But I think this is true, all the same. The Socialists are the strongest advocates of German unity; the loudest opponents of the Schumann plan; the bitterest antagonists of the German Contract and the European Defence Treaty. They are good Socialists, too: their home policy demands a full employment policy, a national health service, a more equitable distribution of wealth and the socialization of the basic industries – in other words, measures advocated by all Social Democratic parties. It may be argued, of course, that German Socialists oppose the Schumann plan because they regard it as Conservative-Capitalist and condemn the European Defence Treaty because they stand for the 'Great Europe' idea (which would include Great Britain and Scandinavia, too) as opposed to the 'Little Europe' idea. Yes, it may be said that they oppose these measures because they are good Socialists and not bad ones. These are fair arguments and there may be some truth in them; but I am convinced that the Socialists – with the exception of the neo-Nazis – are the most Nationalistic party in Germany and whatever they say, they stand on firm nationalistic grounds. This is not a crime; but I feel they should admit it if it is so.

What is the reason for this excessive, or at least very strong, Nationalism of the Great Social Democrats? The explanation is simple. After the first world war the German Socialist Party was the most internationally-minded Social Democratic party in the world. They were reproached for that by the Nazis and called traitors to the fatherland. The Nazis may have been wrong in condemning internationalism but their censure appealed to the German people, including, it seems, most Social Democrats. The policy of the present party leadership is the result of a simple process of over-compensation. As they committed the mistake of being the most internationalist party in the nineteen-twenties, it is only clear that now they have to commit the mistake of being the most nationalistically minded Social Democratic party and all the crimes of the past will be forgiven. They are a progressive party, so they prefer new mistakes to old ones.

Before I went to Germany, I had a long talk on the subject of German Socialists with a prominent member of the British Labour Party. He did not trust the German Socialists, he said, and summarized the reasons for his mistrust in one sentence: 'They are Germans first and Socialists afterwards.' 'While you are Britons first and Socialists afterwards. And this makes a great difference,' I told him. He pondered over this for half a minute, then said: 'Well, it does, doesn't it?'

I quoted this remark to two German Socialists who belong to the top dozen of the Party. One vehemently contradicted his British comrade's suggestion. It was utterly untrue, he exclaimed. This criticism applied to the British Party, not the German. But the other agreed with it: 'Naturally' – he said – 'we are Germans first and Socialists only afterwards. The same applies, with the obvious modification, to all the Socialist parties of the world. Why do you say it's wrong?' 'I never said a word about my own views' – I replied. 'But you obviously imply that it's wrong.' 'I have not implied anything, for the very simple reason that I should not be able to formulate the problem in this simple way. But I have great regard for your own views.' 'Yes, and I hold to them firmly' – he said, and looked at me menacingly. 'Have you said so in public?' 'I have not' – he exclaimed proudly.

The man whose opinions I shall now set down, belonged to smaller fry. He had some, indeed great, local importance on a 'Land' level but did not belong to the upper hierarchy of the Party. He is also an expert on Trade Unions, so I asked him first about Trade Unionism in Germany. He told me the following:

Trade Unions are organized on a non-political basis. Workers of all parties belong to the Trade Unions and

these organizations are strictly forbidden to indulge in
political activities. This is nonsensical because Trade
Unions fight as much for political as for economic aims.
Their political objects are, or should be, (a) stopping the
Ruhr barons from capturing decisive economic influence,
(b) excluding Nazi influence. After the collapse in 1945,
Trade Unions were recognized first on a local basis but
now they are a nation-wide organization, counting six
and a half million members. Of these roughly 65 per cent
belong to the Socialist Party and 35 per cent to the right-
wing democratic parties. Consequently the Social Democrats have the decisive say in all matters but it has never
yet happened that the Unions have been divided on party
lines. The Trade Unions have achieved great successes in
connexion with the Ruhr, i.e., in the vitally important
steel, iron and coal industries. They have great influence
on the boards and now they are fighting for 'co-determination', which means an equal say with the managements in
all these industries.

Trade Union influence inside the Socialist Party is
much less than in Britain. In fact, it is very small. The
reason for this is twofold. First, it is personal. The Trade
Unions have no outstanding personalities strong enough
to influence S.P.D. (Socialist Party) policy on a national
level. This is mostly due to the non-political character of
Trade Unionism; those who seek influence in politics
avoid the Unions. The second reason is economical. Before Hitler, the Trade Unions supported, almost main-
tained, the Socialist Party. All election expenses were paid
by the Unions. Today, one of the most important political
consequences deriving from the non-political nature of
the Unions is that the Party cannot and does not get one
single penny from the Unions. The S.P.D. has become a
poor party and most of its deputies and officials have a

hard struggle. Some of their most influential Members of Parliament cannot even afford a secretary.

The situation of the German workers is good. All who are in employment receive good wages and working conditions are satisfactory. Registered unemployed receive support – enough to live on. Workers enjoy paid holidays, from eight to twenty-four days. Young workers and women have all their necessary rights secured. There are, however, certain kinds of workers who are not properly organized; agricultural labourers, waiters, hotel-employees, domestic workers and, most important, white collar workers. Clerks set themselves above manual workers and a large proportion of them keep away from the Unions, for purely snobbish reasons. They are badly off and that is why these people are dangerous. If Nazism is ever to revive in Germany, it will come as the revolution of the clerks. The white collar workers are split among themselves. About 600,000 of them belong to the Trade Unions, 350,000 have formed their own association and many do not belong to any organization at all. It must be added that the Trade Unions, too, are to be blamed for this state of affairs. They are doctrinaire and dogmatic, they do not welcome white collar workers and if the latter join the Unions, they are often received coolly and regarded with unfriendliness.

This is the gist of what my informant said to me, in answer to my innumerable questions. Then I returned to some of the points raised.

'What do you think about the Ruhr barons?' I asked. 'I thought their influence was not decisive under Hitler.'

'That is true. It was great but not decisive. They used to have much more power under the Weimar Republic. But then as now, they had huge fortunes and fortunes mean power. The Ruhr dies hard. A further trouble is that the Americans simply love them. For them every industrial tycoon is an angel and a good democrat because he is an anti-Communist.'

I asked him some questions about his views on S.P.D. politics.

'The great difference between the C.D.U. (Christian Democratic Union) and the S.P.D. is that the former has electors without having party-members (they have about 100,000 members in all) while the Socialist Party has many members without being a real party. The S.P.D is over-centralized, authoritarian and autocratic. There is no real discussion on any subject.'

'But do you approve the general line of the party?'

'I don't. The Party should know that futile opposition leads nowhere. It is not enough to oppose everything the government is doing.'

'If you are referring mainly to the Party's opposition to rearmament – what policy would you yourself suggest?' I asked.

'It is not my personal view I am going to give you now. Trade Union leadership said *yes* to the rearmament proposition, with certain conditions. We claimed (1) equal rights for Germany with all other participants, (2) co-determination (as outlined above) and (3) that the cost of maintaining the occupation and the expense of the refugees should be borne by the European Defence Organization. I repeat, this was the view of the Trade Union leadership; the rank and file were under the influence of the Social Democratic Party and rejected the proposal of rearmament outright.'

'So you are for rearmament – provided your conditions are fulfilled?'

'No. I should accept it with a heavy heart, but only under the conditions listed. It is true that rearmament would decrease unemployment. Germany has a million and a half unemployed and this is our gravest problem. Rearmament would mean full employment and a rise in the workers' standard of living and I am, naturally, all for it. But, you see, fighting unemployment by a rearmament programme is not very attractive. It smells of evil memories. A man called ...'

'Yes, I remember the name' – I interrupted. 'Do you agree with your party's methods and theories on the problem of German unity?'

'I don't. It is all linked up with the question of rearmament. In fighting the East we must really have a better standard of living than they have. We have it at the moment but the East Zone has touched the rock bottom and will slowly rise from it. If the West sinks at the same time, there will be an equalization of standards and we shall have nothing to offer to the East.'

'That is very interesting. But from all that – if you forgive me for saying so – I do not see where you differ from your Party's line.'

'They use the word "Unity" as a propaganda-slogan. They want to be the best Germans. They are not sincere in this question. They harp on it for political reasons. It is a wonderful vote-catching phrase. Then, the major part of the former Socialist electorate is over in the Eastern Zone. Unity – they think – would mean many voters for the party and an electoral victory of Socialism.'

'Well, they are not the first party in the history of mankind who wish to achieve victory and propagate an otherwise wholly creditable aim partly for selfish reasons.'

'I know. But I think they are wrong even in that. If unity is achieved, the electorate would turn strongly nationalist. Secondly, how can they hope for an electoral victory? Do you think that the Russians – even if they agree to the unification of Germany – will allow an election in which the Social Democratic Party could be victorious? I don't. And I am convinced that the majority of our party leaders don't believe it either.'

'One last question: Is Communist influence strong?'

'No. Except for certain small districts. The Russians are too near. We know too much about them and people are afraid of them.'

We were silent for a while. Then I asked him:

'You disagree with the official party line in all essentials?'

'I do.'

'And have strong doubts on many others?'

'I have.'

'Have you ever said so in public?'

'Never.'

'Will you ever say so?'

'Never.'

'Why?'

'Well – perhaps because I am a good Socialist.'

'But is it the duty of a good Socialist to let his Party do things and take vitally important steps he considers wrong?'

He shrugged his shoulders.

'You know how it is.'

'I don't' – I said, I am afraid a little impatiently. He fell silent again.

'Would you voice your opinion' – he asked me – 'if you were a German Socialist?'

'That I don't know.'

He smiled:

'Because I would voice mine if I were a British Socialist.'

Maybe it is all as simple as that?

Refugees

I DO not wish to tell the reader all about the various political parties and introduce him to all the shades of political opinion in Germany. But I believe a few general observations may not be out of place.

I have said – and repetition may be tiresome but it is not always useless – that the tone of insincerity in German politics struck me very unfavourably. I think, if we are worried about anything in connexion with the Germans, we should worry about this attitude. It is nowhere so conspicuous as in connexion with the problem of German unity. Well, German unity is a sacred aim and everybody pays lip-service to it. Not one single person would have the courage to stand up and declare that he is against it. But many people are, in fact, against it; others view its prospect with misgivings; others again with grave doubts – but all advocate it with zeal and enthusiasm, often *because* it seems to be unattainable.

The unification of Germany is a natural desire. No one likes to see his country divided into two hermetically sealed halves. Of course, the Germans are also unhappy about this state of affairs. What do they have then against unity? First of all, they are afraid of the Russians. Unification would mean increased Russian influence and they dislike the idea. Then various people have various other objections – inspired by their special and personal points of view. East Germany is mainly agricultural and poor, West Germany is industrial and rich, so unification would mean a levelling down for the West. The Christian Democratic Union is closely connected with the Roman Catholic Church and it is the division of Germany that made the Federal Republic a predominantly Catholic state. Unification would make it overwhelmingly Protestant once again by bringing back the Protestant Prussians. The political influence of the Church is enormous. (The English rarely understand political Catholicism. It is the priests who tell people how to vote, what pictures to see, what kind of books to read and what kind of food to eat. The *raison d'être* of the F.D.P. is that many people wanted an anti-clerical, or at least non-Catholic Christian Democratic Party. But there certainly is one layer which is quite satisfied with this great influence of the Catholic Church. It is the Catholic Church itself.) The Social Democrats are the keenest of all on unity, because by losing the Eastern half of the country they have lost their most important electoral districts. But they, too, have their doubts about their policy, as we have seen. Finally, the refugees are also against unification. Many of them would rather see their families reunited in the West, than the country reunited under inevitably increased Russian influence. 'War is the only way to unite the country without getting into Moscow's grasp' – I heard from many refugees – 'and we don't want war. If the choice is between war or non-unification we choose non-unification.'

The refugee question is one of the burning political problems of the day. For some unknown reason, most people accept the idea that being a refugee is not a pain-ful economic plight but a political faith. The Refugee Party is a well organized force but it is dissatisfaction which holds it together. If a Social Democrat or a Nazi becomes a refugee, one would expect him to remain a Social Democrat or Nazi, but he is supposed to become a refugee – a refugee, not by bad luck, but a refugee by con-viction. No political party is a real political party unless its ultimate aim is to gain political power. But even the most rabid refugees do not go as far as to aim at that.

But the refugees are not perfectly united. Some Social Democrats, or Christian Democrats or others remain what they used to be before. They do not become Refugees, only refugees. Others are absorbed by the local popula-tion, and acquire small jobs or major positions and thus cease to be refugees. The unfortunate people in the northern camps and those who live in air-raid shelters are the real problem children. They are miserable and dan-gerous; they deserve assistance because they are badly off but they do not deserve a say in the country's affairs just because they are badly off. There are, of course, a number of professional refugees, too – refugees not by conviction but by trade. Even they do not claim the establishment of a government of refugees, by refugees and for refugees; but they wish to live as refugees, for the refugees and on the refugees. Again others use this pressure group for their own political ends: let the refugees form a group so long as *they* can apply the pressure. But it should be added that it would be unfair to accuse all the people who concern themselves with the refugees' well-being of bad faith. If the Refugee Party is a political party it needs employees, officials and leaders.

There is not much brotherly love wasted on the refu-gees. A refugee is a nuisance; it may be an innocent nuisance, a pitiable nuisance, a nuisance deserving sympathy – but a nuisance all the same. Britain opened her gates to many refugees before the war and on the whole behaved extremely generously to them; but he who thinks that the British people loved refugees, were keen on refugees and were eager to have as many of them as would condescend to honour these shores is committing a grave mistake. In Germany, it is in the North that refugees congregate in large numbers but it is in the South, particularly in Bavaria, where they are most unwelcome. They are unwelcome for three main reasons: (1) they are organized as refugees while the natives are not organized as natives; (2) they take away jobs from the natives in a country where unemployment figures are high. In some parts of the country they are even better off than the natives. In Cologne, for instance, natives are not allowed to move into the city unless they can prove that they have a job there; refugees are free to enter. (3) The greatest objection to the refugee is, however, that they *are* refugees.

The Diplomat

HE is a youngish man, well under fifty. He spent all his working life in the Foreign Ministry, serving in Germany as well as abroad. I think he was a member of the Nazi Party but he probably could not help that. Civil servants had no choice. A refusal to join would have been a meaningless and unnoticed sacrifice. I am not quite certain that he *was* a member. When I asked him, he gave an evasive and diplomatic reply – and I can only presume that, if he had not been a member, his answer would have been a loud and emphatic 'no'. At the beginning of our conversation he was cautious and reserved. He did not trust me far and weighed his words carefully. Later, however, he warmed up and spoke with apparent sincerity and conviction, never stopped to look for a phrase and made no effort to couch his answers in diplomatic phraseology. He was a clever and shrewd man and I could not quite decide whether his sincerity was real or cleverly rehearsed. When we came to the end of our chat, I saw that, judging by the content of his discourse, I had no reason to doubt that he had really spoken his mind. This is what he said.

'Our problems are insoluble' – he started. 'At least insoluble on a short-term basis. We cannot and will not accept the *status quo* – the division of Germany – and at the moment there is only one way of putting an end to it: war. And we do not want war.'

'Why?' I asked naïvely.

'We have learnt our lesson. We lost two wars. We were thoroughly licked. We could not win wars when we had a much larger population than we have today – when we could draw on the population of a united Germany. Now eighteen million Germans live under Russian rule. We could win no wars when we had a magnificent army. Today the German Grand Armée is buried under Russian snow.'

He stopped but I said nothing.

'We are tired of wars' – he went on. 'We do not even want an army. We are prepared to create one – it may be part of the price we have to pay if we wish to be accepted by the West, but we don't want it. The idea of an army is connected with the idea of war–and we are afraid of wars.'

He lit a cigarette.

'We used to say that the "strong is strongest alone". That's rubbish. We were soundly beaten twice. Today we are not strong but we are alone. We have to join the West and the West is an expensive club. Both the entrance fee and the membership fee are very high. But we've got to pay it. We have no strength to deal with France, for instance, so we must make concessions.'

'One day you may join the other club' – I said.

'The Eastern club, you mean? Oh, no – we know Soviet Russia too well. Eighteen million Germans live under Soviet rule. But I know that the suspicion of a new

Rapallo policy lingers in many Western minds. If we are firm with the Russians, the outside world says: These wretched Germans are trying to start a new war. If we are not firm, people say: These wretched Germans are out for a new Rapallo.'

'But is Rapallo out of the question?'

'I never said so' – he protested (although he had). 'Why should it be out of the question? All I say is that it would be idiotic. We cannot afford a balance of power policy – and Rapallo would amount to that. We are too weak for it. Should we try the Rapallo road, it will only lead to a third disaster.'

'But the Germans have always flirted with the idea of a Russo-German alliance. It has a mystic fascination for many' – I told him. 'Together, they think they can conquer the world. German intelligence and Russian manpower. The Germans trust their superior intelligence and are confident that they will not be absorbed by Russian power. They could not conquer Russia by force of arms; what about conquering it with subservience? It's so much easier; and less conspicuous.'

'Some people may have such ideas in mind. But generally speaking, fear is stronger than any faith in our superior intelligence, thoroughness and industry. We are really afraid, maybe for the first time in our history. And this is going to do us a lot of good.'

'Is there no one who wants war?' I asked.

'There are eighteen million Germans who do want war. All the people in the Eastern zone. They clamour for a war of liberation, although they know only too well what war means. But they are desperate. They have been living under Russian rule for a long time now and they have had enough. But – important and dangerous as this may be – this is the only factor of instability.'

'Will the Russians start a war?'

'All our experts agree that they will not. The West must be firm but not provocative. Then the Russians will never start a war.'

'And the Americans?'

'That I don't know. All things considered, I think not.'

'What is then your long-term solution?' I asked. 'You don't accept the *status quo*, you say that war is the only way out of it and you are strongly against war.'

'Our view – that is, the official view – is based on long-term hopes and calculations. For another eight or ten years we must accept the present situation. Then a genuine East-West settlement may become possible. The Russians may agree to unification on proper terms – if all their fears and suspicions are dispelled. We may be disappointed in our hopes, but there is no other way.'

I changed the subject and asked him whether he thought Nazism was dead in Germany.

'Not altogether. Internally and for the Germans the National Socialist government was not so bad. It created a social and economic standard which it is difficult to surpass. I think the Führer-principle was the real curse of Nazism. No one was allowed to think; everyone had to obey all orders blindly. Everyone was responsible to the Führer alone. . . . To Hitler, I mean.'

He stood up and started pacing up and down in the room.

'Put individual responsibility on people's shoulders and that will solve many problems. After all, democratic institutions are as old in Germany as in any other country. There was a sad and very serious rupture, no doubt, but our so-called re-education does not have to start from scratch. Patriotism seems to be a crime today – but we are not prepared to accept this theory. Prussian drill was also regarded as a terrible menace to the world and I had no brief for it. But after the outbreak of the Korean war, to many Western people somehow it does not seem quite as bad as before.'

I did not need to prompt him with questions any more. Our conversation had turned into a monologue.

'The greatest trouble is that fatigue and disillusion have become dominant. None can deny that rebuilding has gone on on a magnificent scale and that is a great help. Millions of housewives have regained their "kitchen-independence" – and this is more important to them than political independence. But, on the whole, the German people are disillusioned. The greatest shock is the shadow of a new war which is hanging over our heads. But there are other shocks, too.'

He stopped as if to consider whether he could speak freely to me. He went on after a very short pause.

'The German army started retreating in 1941 and particularly in the latter stages of the war the army was defending first our frontiers, then our soil. That gave the impression to many that the war was in self-defence; a sacred war for the integrity of the fatherland. Memories were short, as always, and people were quick to forget how it all started. Then, our people believe that it was really the Americans who brought the Russians to the Elbe. Not a very intelligent conception, I admit, but a pretty general one.'

I began to realize what he was driving at.

'After 1945' – he continued – 'the Germans were prepared to accept moral judgement. The truth became too obvious. We have committed mass murders. We massacred hostages. We started the war. But six months after the end of the war the pendulum began to swing and it has been swinging ever since.'

Impatience, even passion, crept into his voice.

'The moral pretensions of the Allies broke down. Hundreds of thousands of Germans were expelled from the Eastern zone: looting was not general but certainly not infrequent; Allied soldiers were engaged in black market deals; thousands of women raped by the Russians; concentration camps were opened; large masses of people condemned not for individual crimes, only for having belonged to certain organizations; Western police were beating up and torturing Germans; our generals were in prison for crimes in partisan warfare while whole villages in Korea are burnt down in reprisal.'

His moral indignation was impressive. He obviously meant every word of it. I did not wish to argue with him but now I had to say something to keep the conversation alive.

'Even if all this were true,' I said, 'do the Allied crimes equal the German ones? Or do they exonerate them?'

He knew that he had said more than he intended. But it was too late to retreat and he was carried away.

'No,' he replied, still softly and politely, but with passion in his voice. 'They don't equal them – but surely that has nothing to do with the moral part of the question. And they do not exonerate them. But we feel ... yes, we feel that we may have been swine but they are swine, too.'

'And this is the conclusion of your analysis of post-war German foreign policy?'

He eyed me furiously. Then he replied with perfect calmness and courtesy:

'We bear no hatred. Someone must begin to take up a more sensible attitude. Hatred must disappear from this world.'

I felt much relieved. He was ready to forgive us, after all.

The Ruhr Barons

WHO rules Germany? – I asked myself many times during my journey. I remembered blood-curdling stories about the Ruhr Barons, those notorious and sinister wire-pullers and back-room boys who stayed in the darkness and started world wars from there. My political outlook makes me naturally hostile to them. I was brought up in an era when it was absolutely compulsory to be a left-wing intellectual and I had to work long and hard before I managed to become a left-wing un-intellectual (which is today's fashion, unless, of course, you happen to be under 60 and choose to be a young conservative). Yes, my political conscience strongly opposes the Ruhr Barons but as an individual – I mean, not in my capacity as a voter but in my capacity as a student of history – I could not fail to be impressed by a man who started a war, however small it may have been. In fact, I always wanted to become a millionaire myself and only the new taxation laws made me change my mind. There was a long time in my youth when I regarded the armament-manufacturers as no more than the villains of modern fairy tales. I read Shaw's preface to *Major Barbara* as I had read the Grimm Brothers' tales ten years before. It seemed to me unfair to blame the boys who produced arms for all our folly. It is so easy to defend yourself against people who manufacture guns and try to sell them – no more difficult than to defend yourself against people who manufacture chewing gum and try to sell it. Don't buy their goods.

I always thought that rearmament and the profit motive had much less to do with each other than was emphasized by my forbear, that early left-wing intellectual, Karl Marx. Individual profits are either good or bad, but if bad then profit on chewing gum or butter is just as obnoxious as profit on guns. Or again, manufacturing arms is either wrong or it is necessary; but if it is wrong, then the rearmament of the Socialist States is not any the less dangerous because no private gains are made in the process.

As I wanted to clear up the mystery of the Ruhr Barons I went to Düsseldorf. The city is called 'little Paris' which it is not. But it was gay, elegant, rich and half in ruins like everything else in Germany. Soon after my arrival I went to a tobacco-shop and asked for a brand of Virginia cigarettes. The man gave me a tin box, containing twenty cigarettes and informed me that its price was eight shillings. He asked me – somewhat contemptuously – whether that was good enough or did I want some better kind of cigarette. As I am an incurable snob and always succumb to the superior attitude of waiters, hotel-porters, doormen and tobacconists, I replied with an equally contemptuous air that I thought I would try the rubbish he was offering me as every now and then I like smoking inferior cigarettes which make me cough. Not too often, though, I added thoughtfully, lest he should think I was not a millionaire. The cigarettes, by the way, had an exquisite flavour and I never found any either as good or as expensive anywhere else in Germany.

The hotel where I met my informant for lunch was the most luxurious, tasteful and beautiful I have ever seen in my life – and that includes the best English, American and Swiss hotels. For lunch we had lobster in aspic, then we had a mixed grill, so tender that you could have spread the meat on a piece of bread (a silly thing to do) and the various vegetables, potatoes and other decorations had been carved by the best sculptors in Germany. We drank white, Rhenish wine with the meal – you could feel the sweetness of sunshine in your mouth – and finished up with *Pêche Melba*, created by Germany's best poet. By the time we reached the coffee I was so demoralized that if my companion had asked me to agree to launching a minor war in Asia, I am not sure what I should have said.

I do not know what my companion's profession was. He was not a Ruhr millionaire but he had something to do with the Ruhr and its millionaires. Unfortunately, you can ask your intimate friends almost any question, except their names and professions. I knew my friend's name – it was a name impossible not to know – and I also knew that he was a charming, witty and well-informed person. I was content with that.

First of all I asked him who could pay eight shillings for a packet of cigarettes apart from me, who had just done so; and who could pay for lunch in that hotel? Many people – he told me. Two years before, there were about eighteen or twenty millionaires in the Ruhr, today there were two hundred. Vast fortunes were made and spent every day. The Korean war had sent prices rocketing up and in Düsseldorf or Essen you could get anything for dollars. Sheets of steel were bought at incredible prices and the sellers, or rather the middlemen, were now parading in huge, chauffeur-driven American automobiles and living in their own central-heated castles. The trouble with German millionaires is that they seem to have taste, which is rather annoying. On the whole, this is a disheartening and repulsive state of affairs. But again, one has to admit that the Korean war was not started by Ruhr – or any other armament – millionaires.

My companion told me about the de-centralization laws – the breaking up of the power of the Ruhr and the great and still growing influence of Trade Unions. He was matter-of-fact and made no comments. The combines had been broken up, the twelve biggest liquidated and re-organized into twenty-eight smaller companies. The administration of the steel and coal industries was in the hands of twelve trustees – these being the highest authorities – and called, rather irreverently, the Twelve Apostles. General Clay appointed these Apostles: four of them are Trade Unionists, four former owners and four independent. Independent of what he did not tell me. The British and Americans set up twenty-three new companies and the boards of these firms consist of three people – there is always one Trade Unionist among them. Eight of the twenty-three boards have Trade Unionists as their chairmen. Co-determination (equal say for the workers' representatives in all production matters) is one of the greatest problems. Some Ruhr firms are resigned to accept it; others say they would rather close down than agree to this. My friend gave me many other details of this nature. I do not want to repeat all the data here, but my final conclusion – reinforced by other, including Labour sources – was that while the Ruhr is still extremely powerful its political influence has greatly diminished. That is, its influence as far as German internal politics are concerned; and for the time being – because the set-backs suffered by the Ruhr Barons may be rectified. But Germany today is run by her government, amazing as it seems. The Ruhr, at the same time, has great importance in the eyes of the Western Allies. The French are afraid of being devoured by the Ruhr, as they have been half-consumed on several previous occasions; the British are afraid of competition on the world markets; the Americans do not really care, but they are aware of the simple fact that a Ruhr millionaire is unlikely to be a Communist. They are aware of the other simple fact, too, that wherever the Ruhr Barons' sympathy may lie, they may be persuaded to sell steel, or anything else, to anyone, quite irrespective of his political creed. For big businessmen anti-Communism is not an ideal, it is simply a way of fighting a remote threat to their business; but nothing is quite so bad for business as not to do it. The Trade Unionists on the boards stop as much of the Iron Curtain dealings as they can; and the new laws make such practices difficult. Should it be found that a Ruhr firm is selling to the East, it is black-listed. Thus, many of the firms are compelled to sell to Russia and her satellites *via* neutral and allied countries. This practice puts the prices up and this is considered an astute political move.

But increasing the price is not the only safeguard for our future. There is another one. We pay compensation to Krupps – after all it was we who bombed his plants. We encourage Krupps and other firms to manufacture armaments. Some silly people frown at this. They do not understand. Were the Ruhr to produce cars, refrigerators and electric toasters, that would cause competition on the world markets and that would be extremely dangerous. So we trick these firms into producing guns, jet-bombers, rockets and other gadgets which cannot be sold on the free market. This is a master-plan to ensure our safety.

The coffee in the hotel was unforgettable. I had a second cup. When we left, my partner pointed out a waiter to me and remarked:

'Should you ever need sheet-steel that waiter can always put you right.'

I do not need sheet-steel just now. But this knowledge made me feel comfortable. It is nice to have my own connexions in the world of high finance.

The Fourth Reich

FOR a long time I could not understand the fine distinction people drew between the neo-Nazis and the old Nazis. Was there a difference in programme and ideology? Or was this only a convenient reference to the vintage year? My guess was – and it was wrong, as guesses usually are – that the new Nazis looked into the future and dissociated themselves from Hitler while the old ones just pondered nostalgically on the glory and beauty of the past and tried to keep alive the memory of the Führer.

But there is no noticeable Hitler cult in Germany. Hitler is dead and gone. I think the psychological story of the Hitler myth is rather interesting and it is a typically German phenomenon. First Hitler turned away from his people, then the Germans turned away from Hitler. One trouble with Hitler was that he was not even a good Nazi. He invented the master-race ideology, filled the Germans' heads with a lot of stuff and nonsense but never really accepted these doctrines. He always despised the masses and believed in the Hero – in himself – in the Nietzschean sense of the word. The conquest of the globe was to be a one-man show – the German people were only an instrument on which he, the greatest artist of all time, was to perform. But when he failed, the failure was blamed on the instrument. He had failed – he said – because the German people proved inferior to his assessment of them and also because they had left the greatest German of all time – as he was fond of briefly referring to himself – in the lurch. They had behaved in a cowardly way – he added – and the German people just did not deserve him. Perhaps they didn't.

The Germans – even the most devoted former followers of their Führer – indignantly reject this explanation. It was Hitler who failed; it was Hitler who did not keep his vainglorious promises and escaped from the consequences of his deeds in a most cowardly fashion. This 'cowardly fashion' is a very strong point in their eyes. They all blame Hitler for his suicide. He ought to have died with a revolver in his hand (funnily enough, nobody ever mentioned a rifle; it is always a revolver) defending the fatherland. They know, of course, that such a gesture would not have made the slightest difference for the fatherland but the Germans have always been formalistic people and the Etiquette for Heroes (§ 107) distinctly says: 'If a Führer plunges his nation into a world war and loses it, he must die fighting with revolver in hand.' Yes, all the former Nazis maintain that to have died like a hero fighting on the barricades would have been admirable and wonderful, while committing suicide and having his corpse burnt was an easy and leisurely way out of his difficulties. A hero must die fighting; the suicide who ordered that his

body should be burnt is considered a hedonist, an epi-
curean, a person devoted to frivolous pleasures and light
entertainment to the very last. 'The Kaiser left us in the
lurch and so did the Führer . . . I mean Hitler' – they
say, dropping a pathetic tear and you can hardly help feeling sorry for the poor fellows.

This reasoning is widely, almost generally accepted in
former Nazi circles. The theory is a life-belt, and with its
help they are trying to perform an ideological and psychological *salto mortale*. One would think that if Hitler was
a hero in someone's eyes, his death made no difference to
the legend; and if he was a despicable and evil creature,
he did not become all that on the day of his death. But he
who reasons this way does not perceive the necessity of the
theory I have described. This theory permits Hitler to
remain a hero until his very last hour – thus justifying his
followers for having stuck to him to the bitter end – and
turns him into a coward and a villain on the day of his
suicide – thus justifying again his former devotees for
having turned away from him at the very moment of his
downfall.

The neo-Nazis are called 'new' because they are the old
ones. I found them disappointing. It was Hitler's evil
genius which made the Nazi Party successful and dangerous. A Nazi-movement without Hitler – or without a
Hitler – is a Chaplin-film without Mr Chaplin. (I hope it
is needless to add that this simile does not imply any com-
parison between that admirable artist and the late German Führer.) The neo-Nazis mostly consist of people
who belonged to the old Nazi gang and their number is
swollen by the malcontents and recalcitrant elements who
are Nazi in every country and under any constitution.
Their phraseology and their uneducated balderdash is an
echo of their predecessor's utterings and they are trying –

not altogether unsuccessfully – to exploit the dissatisfaction of the refugees and other people who are or think they are unfairly treated. I talked to many of them. The one whom I am going to quote addressed me from his arm-chair, as if he had been standing on a huge platform, surrounded by flags and storm-troopers and as if I had been an enthusiastic crowd of 20,000. 'We don't want either the East or the West. We want remilitarization but only under purely German leadership. . . . It is a scandal that generals like Kesselring and Manstein are in prison. The class struggle must be stopped forthwith. Germany must again become the focal point of Europe. Germany must be united. Workers must be consulted on all matters, but they should have no say in the administration of industry.'

The soliloquy continued and he started repeating himself in the best Hitler tradition.

'Germany must be independent. We claim equal rights for all nations. We are not going to be the lackeys of anyone. Neither the East, nor the West . . .' etc., etc.

Tito is one of their heroes. He is the head of a small power which stood up to all pressure. He defied East and West alike (or so I was told). They quote the utterings of Tito and exclaim: 'Have you heard such manly words from the mouth of any German politician since 1945?'

They oppose the German government and they oppose the opposition. They condemn waste – a safe line for all demagogues. 'The present government spends more than the Reich did, including the expenses of the S.A. and the S.S.'

I asked my informant whether he really thought that the Reich was so cheap in the end. I myself – I said – did not regard it as a really good bargain. Instead of replying to that, he remarked that if you drew a line from Helmstedt to Bonn and placed a stone at every two miles, a German minister (this, of course, includes ministers from the *Länder*) could be seated on each stone. They – the neo-Nazi party, called Socialist Reich Party – were no Nazis; it was a slander to call them Nazis. They were true democrats – he went on – and all they wanted was real democratic order. (At the same time, they did not really seem to mind being called neo-Nazis. That was good propaganda, attracting a great deal of attention).

Their leader, Ernst Otto Remer, belongs to a special category. He was the commander of the *Grossdeutschland* regiment at the time of the July attempt on Hitler's life. Remer and his regiment played an important part in putting down the planned revolt and his main interest now is in justifying himself. The Nazis were Germany's legal government – his argument runs – Germany was engaged in a life and death struggle and all who tried to stab her in the back were traitors. For Remer, time stopped in July 1944 – as, indeed, it has stopped at one time or another for many politicians of quite different calibre, standing and mental make-up.

I knew an honest Hungarian statesman who played an important part in 1918 and 1919 in Hungary's politics and still keeps judging people and modern political events from the 1918 angle. Surprisingly enough, if Senator Taft makes a speech in Oklahoma or Moussadek takes a step in the Anglo-Persian oil dispute, all these events seem to have some relation to the 1918 occurrences in Hungary. I had another friend whose great days came at the time of General Gömbös' half-forgotten, semi-fascist, semi-dictatorship. For my friend, history stopped at the mid-thirties and humanity can be divided into two groups: the Gömbösists and anti-Gömbösists. It is no use pleading that you have no idea who the man in question was. Or take our own Sir Winston Churchill. His greatness and immortal services to this country and the whole world are, I believe, beyond dispute. But his finest hour came in 1940, when the eyes and the hopes of the world were fixed on him and he could stand up and had nothing to offer but 'blood, toil, tears and sweat'. Twelve years later, during his second period of office, he could not stop himself from getting up on the slightest provocation, and offering us a little more blood and sweat. It had become force of habit. We have all, more than once, seen Sir Winston get up in the House of Commons to tell the nation that we were heading towards disaster and bankruptcy, drastic measures were inevitable and we would get a new dose of blood and sweat. Soon afterwards his Chancellor has had to explain that what the Premier really meant was that things were rosy although they could have been still rosier. The stern measures referred to turned out to be a new Empire Economic Conference – which may be terrible but which, after all the threats, looked rather an anti-climax. All this does not diminish Sir Winston's greatness or the value of his historic services; but it shows – and it is quite useful that some people should be reminded of it sometimes – that, great man as he is, he too is only human.

Remer's preoccupation with the July attempt is an important monomania. He needs a political movement to justify himself and a neo-Nazi movement at that. In this aspect he resembles Adolf Hitler. Hitler started a world war because some Jews had trodden on his corns, because he was only an Austrian, not a real German, and because he could not rise above the rank of corporal in the army. I am not suggesting that all former Austrian corporals with a grudge against the Jews are equally dangerous; circumstances favoured Hitler and he was a genius of the first magnitude. Remer is not a genius – far from it. But we do not know whether circumstances will support or crush him and whether Germany, Europe and humanity will or will not be called to pay a price to solve his grave doubts concerning the rights and wrongs of his behaviour on a July day in 1944.

In Search of a Nazi

I HOLD no brief for the Nazis. I must declare bluntly that I never liked them. But while I was in Germany, there was a time when I turned towards them with something almost approaching sympathy. The general and universal betrayal of the Nazi cause made me sad and despondent. After all, the Nationalist Socialist Party had had millions of members; it had commanded the enthusiastic loyalty of huge masses. 'Isn't there one single person left in Germany,' I asked myself, 'who says: "I used to be a Nazi; I am a Nazi. I believe the Nazis were right"?' People who tell you that they had always been ardent anti-Nazis and fighters for democracy and individual freedom, may well be speaking the truth; but they may be liars. On the other hand, a man who confesses that he was and still is a Nationalist Socialist needs, at least, a certain amount of courage and conviction.

But for a long time I could not find a Nazi in Germany.

Not one single remnant of so many millions. I looked for them everywhere. I met many people who told me that they knew some Nazis personally or had seen one or two from quite near but when I asked them to produce one, these legendary Nazis always disappeared into thin air. Perhaps they refused to meet me – I thought for a while. But this was no explanation. I met many people who talked to me with great frankness on all matters and, after all, I was looking for one solitary example only – one, left over from so many millions.

I saw many phenomena, reminding me of Nazism. I have already spoken of the neo-Nazi Party. But to call the Socialist Reich Party neo-Nazi is only a convenient and not fully justified term. Anyway, I was looking for an old Nazi, not a new one; I was looking for a self-confessed Nazi and not one labelled Nazi by political opponents. I also knew that in certain public offices – first of all in the Foreign Ministry – many former members of the Nazi Party were still at their posts. But I had no means of investigating this matter properly. No doubt, the actual statement was true. But what did it mean? Very little in itself. Officials of the various ministries had to join the Party whether they liked it or not and we cannot label people who were *forced* to become members of the Party Nazis, without finding out a little more about them. No man in good faith can maintain that Adenauer is prepared to shield Nazis – that is people who did more than formally join the Party. It is also true that competent foreign experts do not grow on every tree and the government had to make concessions. Even the Socialists told me that they were having great difficulties in finding properly trained Trade Union officials as Trade Unionism had been extinct in Germany for twelve years.

Then I saw certain articles in the press which made me frown. I read one, for instance, in a magazine, which drew a parallel between Napoleon III and Hitler. Napoleon III – the article argued – was a dictator, too, acquired power in the same legal or semi-legal way as Hitler did, and used and abused his power in a similar fashion. *Napoléon le petit* was also defeated in a war but thanks to Bismarck's generosity he was not tried as a 'war criminal' (such expressions were always used in inverted commas). According to the Nuremberg laws he ought to have been hanged. Well, if this is not latent Nazi propaganda, I do not know what is. Articles such as this give rise to an outcry and sometimes I was inclined to think that the uproar was partly justified and partly the result of hysteria. It is easy to call many things 'un-German activity'. There were a number of articles published on Magda Goebbels, or Nazi leaders – not praising them openly – but featuring them prominently and publishing their glamorous photographs. Some of these articles are trying to keep the heroes of yesterday before the public eye; but others write of them simply because they are interesting persons to write about and – in certain cases – because one has something new to say about them. After all, books on Rommel, the diaries of Goebbels and the memoirs of Nazi supporters were published also in this country and in the United States and no one in his senses would accuse their publishers that their aim was the spreading of disguised Nazi propaganda.

At last, I thought, I had succeeded in finding my Nazi. In Bonn, I stayed at a hotel in the outskirts of the town, at a place called Beuel on the wrong side of the Rhine bridge. Beuel is a bad address, but the hotel was beautifully situated on the banks of the Rhine; it was clean and cheap and I have always been fond of bad addresses. My arrival in a car with a G.B. plate puzzled the kind and polite proprietor as well as the waiters and all the other guests, as the hotel was not a really international one. The proprietor and the other guests kept putting leading questions to me, trying to find out what kind of bird I was and what I was doing in Bonn. The mystery grew around me when a few well-known personalities or ministries rang me up and left messages. At last I told them that I was a writer in search of material for a book on Germany. From that fateful moment they became oppressively helpful and asked me five times a day whether they could help me. It occurred to me that they could; I wanted to meet a self-confessed Nazi who made no bones about his past. They did help me; they produced the Nazi for me.

We talked on the terrace overlooking the Rhine, in lovely sunshine, sipping beer.

Yes, he had been a Nazi – he told me. The Nazis had done a lot of good. They had given employment for everyone and created order.

'First I was attracted to them,' he said, 'because there was chaos in Germany and I thought it was only the Nazis who were capable of making order and introducing discipline. A dictatorship is good in itself, but when the dictator becomes mad, it is not so good any more.'

'In fact, it must be quite awkward on occasions,' I nodded.

'Yes, this was a great disappointment for me,' he agreed.

I asked him in what circumstances he had joined the Party. Oh, it was an accident, almost a mistake. It occurred in 1932. He had been living then in a small village in the north and had gone to a neighbouring town to listen to the speakers at a Nazi rally, when he was introduced by an S.S. *Obersturmführer* to the audience as the

first member from his village. The audience applauded
and there was nothing to be done about it. He became a
member.

But he turned against the Nazis as early as in 1933 – he
explained. He noticed that winter relief was not allo-
cated with fairness. Some people were refused because
they were church-goers and others because they had been
Communists. That was a terrible disappointment to him
because he thought all Germans should be treated
equally. He was an idealist – he added – just like
the great masses of the German people. People in Germany were not Nazis at all in the sense that people
abroad believed them to be; they became Nazis because
they were idealists. He also objected to some of the
local Nazi leaders because in his view they were not
idealists.

What about the Jews? – I asked him.

Yes, the Jews. Needless to say – he said – he knew nothing about concentration camps. Absolutely nothing. He
knew that there were a few Communists in concentration camps (in concentration camps about which he knew
nothing) but these men were also common criminals. It
was fair to say that (a) he knew really nothing about the
existence of these camps and (b) he always thought that
they were ordinary prisons or even some kind of work-
houses where people were being re-educated, to become
idealists like the rest. He learnt the truth near Dachau in
1945. He even saw some of the prisoners who were terribly
emaciated and had extremely long finger-nails. That
showed that they had never done any work at all. They
refused to do useful work even after having been liberated
and boasted about that openly. Many of these people – he
thought – perhaps most of them, were common criminals.
And in 1945 they were living in comfort and were fed on

butter and eggs and steaks while ordinary Germans had to go about hungry.

'The West keeps talking about "Nazi atrocities",' he went on, 'but has anybody ever seen anything of the kind?' The German army was scrupulously honest and individual looting was severely punished. A corporal he knew had been sent to prison because he could not show the payment receipt for certain goods he had sent home to Germany. Yes, this was how the German army behaved and yet people keep talking about atrocities. He himself was in France with the occupation forces. He had never entered a French home without knocking on the door.

'I understand,' I interjected, 'that even the Gestapo always knocked before entering French homes.'

'You see,' he said, 'even the Gestapo knocked.'

I asked him what he thought about Germany's rearmament.

'We belong to the West,' he answered. 'We must defend our *Kultur*. But we do not want to fight. We fought in the last war but in 1945 we were declared criminals. Why should we fight again? To be called criminals once more? No, thank you.'

I asked him whether he belonged to the Socialist Reich Party – the neo-Nazis – but he protested vigorously. No, he belonged to the F.D.P. – the smaller step-brothers of the Christian Democrats.

'I am a democrat now,' he assured me.

'What caused the change?' I inquired.

'Well, I was dissatisfied with the political situation. I did not like the way things were developing after the war. Former party-members and even former soldiers were discouraged from taking an active part in public life. We were supposed to leave the field to those who were anti-Nazis before 1933 or 1939. That seemed to me all wrong. Why shouldn't we have a say in our country's affairs? So I became a democrat.'

He stopped talking and emptied his glass. Then he turned to me, smiling:

'I know that we are the bogey-men – we former Nazis. But that is quite unjustified. I hope you know better and you are not afraid of us.'

'I am not afraid of old Nazis,' I replied. 'I am only afraid of new democrats.'

Ten Years After

IN PRAISE OF LAZINESS

REVISITING Germany ten years after my first post-war visit, I found myself soon after my arrival taking part in an unexpected and delicious experience.

I stayed the night in Cologne. Here I met two English girls who promised to come along next morning and help me with some shopping. I, in turn, offered to drive them out to Cologne airport, as they were on their way back to London. As the airport serves both Bonn and Cologne, I presumed that it must be situated somewhere between the two cities. This belief was confirmed by the hotel porter and officials of the airport in question.

'Take the Autobahn in the direction of Bonn and follow the signs,' a helpful clerk told me.

We found the Autobahn, all three of us kept our eyes glued on the signposts and soon we arrived alas, not at the airport, but at Bonn. That was about ten o'clock in the morning. Actually I had an appointment in Bonn at 10.20 but there was nothing for it. I had to turn back and look for the airport. We spotted signposts with even more ardour but again in vain: we found ourselves back in Cologne. We played the game in the reverse direction to Bonn just once more; by now we regarded the signposts as a sort of challenge and were determined to beat them. But the signposts won. We had to ask our way and were directed and misdirected by four very kind but not too brilliant local gentlemen. Finally a commercial traveller, heading for Frankfurt, took pity on us and piloted me to the airport: driving in front of me, making a considerable detour. We reached the airport at 11.30, about half an hour after the girls' plane had left. They were put on another plane and, instead of arriving in London at 12.30, they arrived in Copenhagen at 4.58.

Having delivered them at the airport, I set out for Bonn, the capital of Germany. I could not find it.

Following the signposts I reached a large number of other villages but saw no sign of the village of Bonn. At one place which – I was informed – was less than ten miles from the capital, I decided to ring up my friends who were waiting for me but was told that there was no telephone in the village. Having learnt that I was only ten miles from Bonn, I decided to drive on as fast as I could. With the help of the excellent signposting system, aided and abetted by the sympathetic and helpful local population, I managed to cover the last ten miles in just over two hours and arrived in Bonn by ferry boat at 1.17 p.m.

To me this experience was not just thrilling; it was most encouraging. I know so much about German thoroughness, German genius for organization, etc., etc. that it was most refreshing to find German muddle and German incompetence. But was this – I asked myself doubtfully – just a happy coincidence, a pleasant exception or was it a promising sign of genuine change?

I am overjoyed to report that it was indeed a genuine symptom. I had not spent another twenty-four hours in the land before I found out that, in the last ten years, Germany has changed almost as much as Britain.

What a long period in history ten years is! When I first came here, Adenauer was a mere stripling of seventy-six; together he is a mature statesman of eighty-six. Then one of the main problems was the influx of refugees; today everyone complains of the shortage of refugees; not enough of them are getting through and this situation creates a shortage of labour.

In the meantime, we have also had the *Wirtschaftswunder* – the economic miracle. The *Wirtschaftswunder* was the result of the *Furor Teutonicus*, described in earlier chapters of this book; the frenzied force which – so it seemed – made the Germans *fight* in the early forties and made them *work* in the following decade. In the course of a few years a war-stricken, ruined, half-starved Germany was transformed into one of the richest industrial powers of Europe, capturing export markets at alarming speed. When the pound sterling and even the almighty dollar found themselves in grave difficulties, the Germans condescended to *up-rate* the mark, to help the poor former victors in their dire trouble. While strikes were paralysing British, French and other West European industry right and left, the Germans just worked, worked and worked, and produced more and more while their exports forged ahead at the expense of all their competitors.

When the idea of Britain's entry into the Common Market gained popularity in this country, people turned pale. 'How can we compete with those Germans?' they asked trembling. 'They *work*.'

They also travel. Whether you go to Positano or the Costa Brava, to Corfu or Majorca, you hear more German spoken than Italian, Spanish or Greek. The Ticino – the Italian-speaking Canton of Switzerland – has been practically bought up by the Germans. I once asked a friend why he was going to Palma for his holiday. He looked at me uncomprehendingly: 'Well, why does one travel to Majorca? To learn German, of course.'

Soon I understood why the Germans have taken to travel. First, because travelling has become a universal mania of this age. I am bitten by this bug; so are you, Gentle Reader; and so are the Germans whom we should, therefore understand. Travelling has become a new status symbol. In olden days people travelled *in order to get somewhere*: to see, to study, to enjoy new and unknown places. It was the pull of strange and fascinating lands that moved them. Later they travelled to *get away from it all*: it was the push of dreary and tiresome surroundings. Today people travel *in order to return* and wave their trophies – photograph, souvenirs and embroidered Greek skirts – in their neighbours' faces. It is a richochet: they *go in order to come back*, like a master-stroke in billiards. But the Germans have an additional reason for *their* travelling mania. They all have relations or friends in the East but they cannot go to visit them. The man of Frankfurt cannot go to Dresden, so he travels to Rhodes instead. It is easier for a man of Hamburg to go to Tokyo than to Leipzig – so to Tokyo he goes. For a Berliner, living near the Zoo, Sydney is much more accessible than Unter den Linden – less than half a mile away. So he flies to Sydney.

The division of Germany is a tragedy which – even if it is provoked by their own folly – deserves our sympathy. But it has its pleasant sides, too. I personally would not mind if it were easier to go to Tahiti than to Manchester; if Hawaii were more accessible than Stockton-on-Tees; if it were less trouble to get to California from Marylebone than to Commercial Road, E.1. 'Hell,' I should say ruefully and off I would go to Honolulu.

A feeling of guilt has also compelled them to travel. Many of them return to the scene of their crimes: exsoldiers and former S.S. men started taking their wives and children to visit places in Holland and Norway where they once served as members of the occupation forces. They entered their old billets with beaming faces. They were received with coolness at best; more often with hostility; and sometimes they were simply and unceremoniously kicked out. The Dutch and the Norwegians were outraged and thought the Germans had come to gloat; the Germans themselves – well-meaning, stupid people in most of these cases – were also taken aback and shook their heads sadly. They felt their outstretched hand had been rapped, their well-meant friendly approach rebuffed.

It is the case of Mahomet all over again: if Germany cannot go to Europe in certain cases, let Europe come to Germany. That is why they became such genuinely good Europeans; such mainstays of the Common Market. Of course, they have their well-considered economic reasons, too: *but they want to belong to Europe.* They want to be accepted again. They know that much less is said about Nazi crimes today than ten years ago; nevertheless, they want it in writing, that they belong to Europe. They want a big official document, with large red seals.

We all used to think that the Germans' mania for hard work was even stronger than their mania for travelling. But on this count I am able to report a most pleasant surprise. We don't need to worry. This legend ought to disappear and is in fact disappearing fast. The Germans – I am delighted to report – are almost as lazy as the English. They work less than any other European nation and get higher wages, while the quality of their products has fallen. Employers go in fear of their employees; no waiter, for example, is ever told off, however impertinent he may choose to be. In fact, truculent clients are often asked to keep away from restaurants as they may annoy the waiters: the owner knows he can get as many clients as he wants but waiters are few and far between. Customers are kept waiting in stores while assistants finish their little chats. Strikes too are becoming more and more frequent.

I do not paint this picture in order to deride the Germans but, on the contrary, to build them up. If, after the war, they felt an irresistible urge to rebuild their devastated country, and take great pride in the magnificent results, that is perfectly understandable. But after some years this urge has faded. A permanent mania for hard work would be a frightening thing; the desire to shirk is human. Work for work's sake is a repulsive and sinister thing; to get the maximum reward for the minimum of work is a worthy, meritorious and natural desire which we condemn in others but which we all share. The Germans hate work just as much as other decent people do. They are really quite human. They do belong to Europe.

TWO GENERATIONS

During my absence the memory of the Nazi past grew dimmer by ten years. German democracy, an absolute beginner at the time of my first visit, settled down and matured during the decade that followed. When I saw Germany first, she was a country under occupation; a few months before my last visit the British Government had appealed to the German Minister of Economics, begging him to consider and discuss with other members Britain's possible accession to the European Common Market.

All German parties still talk of the Unity of Germany as the primary aim in life and I still do not quite believe them. I am convinced that with the exception of the East Germans and the inhabitants of Berlin, people pay lip-service only to the idea of unification while really they could not care less. In West Germany people are interested in their own lives, in their own affluence, in football, their new cars, but not in unification. They know it ought to be their primary concern; but it isn't. Should you, however, voice this suspicion aloud, everyone will angrily protest. I did not like this attitude ten years ago; I do not like it today. But in the intervening decade I myself grew five or even five and a half years older, and now I understand it better.

Before the war, Revisionism was the order of the day in Hungary. Two-thirds of Hungary's territory had been taken away after World War I, and the Revisionism really meant that we claimed it all back. The Treaty of Trianon (our equivalent of Versailles) was extremely unjust; but this 'we want it *all* back' was silly and pointless. Nevertheless, any politician who would have dared to say that a fair and reasonable compromise, a readjustment of the frontiers would do instead of claiming everything back to the last square inch, would have been hunted out of public life. Of course, no one – except credulous schoolboys and the most gullible readers of the nationalist gutter-press – believed that Hungary could ever get back all her lost territories. But we had to say so; and we did say so.

But Hungary was a semi-fascist, Central European country, one may remark. Very well. I should like to see the politician who would dare to utter republican views in England; and where is the politician, even the budding business executive, brave enough to call himself a

Socialist in the United States? But even if we stick to this particular issue, why blame the Germans? They, at least, would not *mind* re-unification. But we use every opportunity for repeating that the division of Germany is a shame and we must help them to achieve unity. We never add our own thoughts on the subject: how would we like a re-united, sixty million strong Germany as a member of the Common Market and once again by far the strongest power in Europe? It is only the Russians – the staunchest opponents of German unity – who, under certain conditions, would not mind it. They have had to relinquish their hopes of bolshevizing Italy and France; their only hope left is to bolshevize Europe through Germany: to use the Constitution of a reunited Germany for their own purposes and use German reunification as the thin end of the wedge.

It is, indeed, a characteristic comment on our age: none of those who so vociferously call for the reunification of Germany really want it; the only people in favour of it are those who oppose it bitterly.

I was much more perturbed by the Germans' attitude to questions of truthfulness and keeping a promise. I asked one of the leaders of the Free Democrat Party why it was that they had declared 'no coalition under Adenauer' – and the next thing we knew, there was a coalition under Adenauer.

'Oh, but that was only politics . . . tactics, you know,' he said with an innocent smile.

'What do you mean?' I asked a little surprised.

'Well, we wanted to help the Christian Democrats to get rid of Adenauer. We could not pull it off. So we formed a coalition under the old man.'

'But don't you think it is wrong to declare one thing solemnly one day and do the exact opposite the next?'

All he would say about this was:

'It is always a mistake to try and fight other fellows' battles. If they want to get rid of Adenauer, let them do it themselves.'

He did not even see the point of my consternation.

It is not chic today to ask: how dangerous is Germany? How likely is she to become a totalitarian dictatorship and a menace to world? No one asks these questions nowadays but they are, of course, on many people's minds.

I do ask it. And my answer – ten years after my first shot at an answer – is this: there is no danger at all.

Three things have happened since we – Germany and I – last met.

(1) *The Diary of Anne Frank*. I know this is a curious statement but it is nevertheless true. The Germans flocked to see it, wept and were overcome with shame. Perhaps this is as it should be. You cannot grasp what it means to murder 'six million people'. You can understand what it means to murder one clever, brave, innocent little girl and her family. It is quite in keeping that the Germans should finally be more moved and more profoundly convinced by a melodrama, than by the judgements of Nuremberg.

(2) But, of course, they had – sooner or later – to face the six millions, indeed, the twelve millions, too. And it was the *Eichmann case* that made them face it.

For Eichmann they felt only hate and a kind of numb horror. They spent hours every day, while the trial was on, listening to the long stupefying catalogue of horror and sadism and mass-murder. They – and when I say 'they', I mean the overwhelming majority of the Germans with the exception of the hard core of incorrigibles – were utterly indifferent to the fate of Eichmann. The whole story has, at last, been told; Germany listened to it; Germany condemned it. The arch-criminal has been hanged. Scores have been settled, crimes expiated. All sheets are clean now.

(3) But the most significant development of these past ten years is the fact that *a new generation has grown up.* If we take only those people who were born in 1933, the year Hitler came to power, and who could not possibly be blamed for the advent of the Nazis – these people form about 23 per cent of the total German population. If we add three more age groups to these – all those born in or after 1928, the oldest of whom were five years old when the Nazis took over and seventeen when the Führer's dead body was burnt in the Berlin bunker – we have about one third of the total population of Germany who are about as responsible for Hitler as present day Frenchmen are for Napoleon. And there is a deep cleavage between the old generation and the new. This is a serious and significant phenomenon. *'How could you?'* these young people ask their elders in genuine horror and disgust; and their parents cannot give an answer. A few of them are defiant; some are repentant; some shrug their shoulders or talk about Versailles, unemployment and the Communist danger. But most of them look down and cannot reply to the youngsters or themselves. Yes, how could they? How could anyone? They do not know. The youngsters know that their fellow countrymen are essentially decent people; they know that their own feelings and reactions are all right. They also know that other countries, too, have their Hitlers, Himmlers and Kaltenbrunners – psychopaths, sadists, maniacal killers. But in other countries such characters are locked up in criminal lunatic asylums while *their* Daddies and Mummies elected them to rule the land. Why?

The Eichmann trial might have been expected to make an impact on the young and bring the truth home to them. But, I fear, both in Israel and in Germany, the young generation is more bewildered than enlightened. Young Israelis feel contempt for their elders for not resisting their sadistic murderers and tormentors; young Germans feel contempt and hatred for the murderers, who may be their parents, teachers, employees. They fail to understand it; and their questions remain unanswered.

Germany today is as genuinely democratic a country as the rest of Western Europe. No, there is no danger of German Nazism or neo-Nazism. But the fruits of disillusion and cynicism are ripening. There is danger of nihilism. There is no danger of Nazism.

The final proof of genuine change is in the German language itself. Whenever a nation starts ranting about 'blood and soil' and spouting mystical and mythical nonsense, the danger is always grave. Today, few Germans utter the word 'Vaterland' without blushing; indeed, few Germans utter the word 'Vaterland' at all. To move to the purely private plane, even love declarations have become quiet, hesitant, unromantic. No kneeling in front of the beloved; no words like 'forever': the era of the vague understatement has arrived in Germany. The grand words of patriotism, the romantic image and searing rhetoric belong today to General de Gaulle.

A nation which refuses to use resounding, empty phrases and heroic or mythical clichés may have many faults but it is certainly not dreaming of national grandeur and totalitarian tyranny. When the first bombastic orator gains the ear of a German audience, the world will be well advised to pick up its ear in turn. At the moment such a man would be hooted out of Germany.

THE WORLD OF OLGA SEGLER

'Have you seen the Wall?' the airline official asked me, on the way from the tarmac to the hall.

'First we'll go and see the Wall,' said the pleasant young man who was waiting for me at the airport. 'Immediately after lunch.'

'Have you seen the Wall yet?' the hotel receptionist inquired when I signed the book.

I remembered another country I had visited after ten years' absence: Israel. There everybody asked me in equally expectant tones: 'Have you seen our new Concert Hall? It's said to be the best in the world.' The Berliners – I could not help getting rid of the churlish feeling – were as proud of their Wall as the Israelis were of their new Concert Hall. 'Have you seen the Wall? It is said to be the best in the world.'

Immediately after lunch we did go to see the Wall, which is a monstrosity, in every sense of the word. There are, on the Western side, little wooden platforms from which people look over to the East and shake hands. Eight out of ten utter one single word:

'Wahnsinn.' Or in English: 'Sheer madness.'

On the other side you see very little or nothing. A few Vopos – Communist policemen with bren guns – a few sullen-faced passers-by, but all at some distance because there are about 300 yards of no-man's land between the Wall and the life of East Berlin. At some points there are houses on the boundary: all evacuated, all empty and derelict, all doors and windows walled in and all looking like eerie ruins from the more nightmarish stories of Edgar Allan Poe. You listen for the hooting of owls. Almost thirty miles of this hideous obstacle run through the middle of the city.

Some people chalk slogans on the grey wall. 'K.Z.' is the most frequent, the abbreviation for the German word meaning 'concentration camp'. Others write more defiant phrases such as: 'THERE'S ONLY ONE BER-LIN!' As you drive along the endless Wall you see, here and there, strange-looking, little, improvised memorials: wooden sticks put together, holding some candles and a few wreaths and memorial notices. The first I saw – in the Bernauer Strasse – was as follows:

'31.7.81	OLGA SEGLER	+ 26.9.61.'

In other words, Olga Segler, born on the 31st July 1881 died on that spot on the 26th September 1961. After some brief reckoning you realize that Mrs Segler was eighty years old. And you are told that she died because when trying to jump down from the fifth floor of a building on the other side she missed the tarpaulin held out by the West Berlin Fire Brigade. The wreaths commemorate the very spot where her broken body lay on the pavement. There are quite a few of these memorials: young men and old ladies, middle-aged men and little children – who jumped and missed. You read the first few inscriptions and then accept them as part of the landscape and pay no more attention.

Then you go back to Berlin and try to forget about the Wall. During my first visit to Germany I tried to find a Nazi but did not succeed. This time I tried to find a Prussian but failed even more miserably. Here, in the former capital of Prussia, in the province of Brandenburg, you cannot find one single person who would proudly and defiantly – or modestly and blushingly – call himself a Prussian. 'Prussian' may have become a dirty word for many, but after all, Prussians are a great and powerful nation – a nation rich in past glory and great achievements – yet they are extinct. This is another of Hitler's achievements: instead of exterminating the Jews, he managed to wipe the Prussians off the face of the earth.

I had looked forward to seeing Berlin again – it was the one German city I ever fell in love with. Our meeting, as so often happens when erstwhile lovers meet again, was a disappointment. The defiant, gloriously radiant mocking spirit of Berlin was gone. When I was last there, Berlin still reflected the spirit of its finest hour – the Blockade; today it is a neurotic city. I do not blame the Berliners for this. If I lived there I would share that neurosis. You cannot be defiant, brave, and indomitable for years on end. One understands it all. You sympathize with the Berliners. Yet, their monomania gets you down. For them, there is only one problem in the world: Berlin. All other problems are merely peripheral to this central issue. There is no subject, no discussion in West Berlin which does not end up in discussing the Wall and Ulbricht and the future. It all reverts to 'August 13th' – (of 1961) – the day the city was divided. You still admire their spirit; but today they *expect* you to admire it. 'We *are* brave, aren't we?' they seem to ask you. 'Oh, yes, you are,' you murmur.

Berlin has also shrunk in the meantime. In size, first of all: it has been cut in half. But spiritually even more so. 'We are the only metropolis of Germany,' they emphasize several times a day. The truth is that the city has grown rather provincial. It is small; it is cut off from its natural background; everyone who comes to Berlin acquires 'distinguished visitor' status and Berlin is grateful. They are photographed standing by the Wall. A real metropolis does not care who comes and goes; a real metropolis does not emphasize that it is a metropolis any more than old Rockefeller or Ford would have emphasized that he could afford a new suit every month. Berlin chic, Berlin elegance became a bit shrill; they really feel that they have been left out in the cold.

Berlin still has its charm and spirit. Berliners know that the West will not let them down and that 'NO WAR OVER BERLIN' is just an empty slogan of the Western Communists. The West may or may not love the Berliners – it does rather like them, their behaviour during the Blockade endeared them to many hearts – but the West cannot start this 'letting down' process. It would smell of Munich; it would break their spirit. You let down two and a half million Berliners today and then – why not? – four and a half million Danes tomorrow. And so on.

Yes, you still enjoy being in Berlin. ... You tell yourself that the Opera is wonderful; no German town has a comparable theatrical life; Berliners are brave, spirited, they are wonderful; perhaps Berlin, after all, *is* the only metropolis of Germany. 'I love Berlin, it deserves it' – you go on shouting and dare not contradict yourself .

And then, suddenly, the utter idiocy of the situation becomes clear to you. You realize that just as Hitler, as I described earlier in this book, achieved exactly the opposite of all his aims, the same procedure is still going on. The East Germans, by building this monstrosity, the Wall, which upsets West Berliners and the rest of us so much, really solved – at least temporarily – the Berlin question. They did a tremendous favour to the West. This is, of course, a Wall of Shame, as far as they are concerned. They had to seal East Berlin off, otherwise the Communist Paradise would have been bled white of workers and young people. But once this Wall of Shame has been built, once the young people cannot come over (apart from a trickle here and there) the Berlin question has lost its urgency.

On the other hand, the West is playing the East's game, too. By showing off with their Wall, by exhibiting that curiosity as an old Balkan beggar exhibits his wounds; by treating it as a sightseeing attraction for foreigners, the Berliners keep up a crisis atmosphere, keep West German and foreign capital away and proclaim what Ulbricht — if not the Russians — wishes them to proclaim: there is a crisis here, a burning problem which might explode at any moment.

You shake your head sadly. Let's try to understand. Here we are, in a world where there is a Western city in the middle of a Soviet Ocean. This city is the capital of one German state, but half of it belongs to another German state. There is a wall between the Eastern and the Western parts of this city. Translated into London or New York terms, this means that someone who tries to go from Fleet Street to Trafalgar Square or from Fifth Avenue East Side to Fifth Avenue West Side is committing a crime for which he can be tortured, imprisoned or shot. This situation has become so indispensable for one side that it might be bad, but nothing can be done about it.

And then, once again, you think of Olga Segler. We have created a world, where old ladies of eighty jump out of fifth floor windows, not because the house is on fire but simply because they're ready to risk their lives to be able to spend their last few years a few streets away in the same city. Olga Segler — blessed be her memory! — who jumped from the fifth floor and missed the tarpaulin is a tragi-comic symbol of our tragi-comic times.

MORE ABOUT PENGUINS

Penguinews, which appears every month, contains details of all the new books issued by Penguins as they are published, From time to time it is supplemented by *Penguins in Print* – a complete list of all our available titles. (There are well over three thousand of these.)

A specimen copy of *Penguinews* will be sent to you free on request, and you can become a subscriber for the price of the postage – 4s. for a year's issues (including the complete lists). Just write to Dept EP, Penguin Books Ltd, Harmondsworth, Middlesex, enclosing a cheque or postal order, and your name will be added to the mailing list.

Some other Penguins by George Mikes are described overleaf.

Note: *Penguinews* and *Penguins in Print*
are not available in the U.S.A or Canada

More by Mikes

ITALY FOR BEGINNERS

In *Italy for Beginners*, George Mikes writes with a flagrant disregard for guide-book conventions to give you the inside information on Italy you really want to know . . .

How the Living help the Dead; How to be Kicked out of a Job; Two Redeeming Sins; Prices, Hotels, Women; a portmanteau guide to any Italian cathedral and any Italian town . . . Highlights of a humorous classic in the inimitable Mikes manner.

LITTLE CABBAGES

Little Cabbages tells you more about getting around France and getting on with the French than a shelf-ful of more conventional guide-books.

The lowdown on losing your way; being Decadent; sex; sitting in cafes; 'Merde-alors-ism'; the three National Passions, and much more – including some astringent asides on perfidious Albion!

And

HOW TO BE AN ALIEN

HOW TO BE INIMITABLE

HOW TO SCRAPE SKIES

HOW TO TANGO

HOW TO UNITE NATIONS

MORTAL PASSION

Not for sale in the U.S.A.